cloth hats, bags 'n baggage

cloth hats, bags 'n baggage

DOROTHY FRAGER

CHILTON BOOK COMPANY
Radnor, Pennsylvania

Published in Radnor, Pa., by Chilton Book Company
and simultaneously in Don Mills, Ontario, Canada,
by Thomas Nelson & Sons, Ltd.
Manufactured in the United States of America

Library of Congress Cataloging in Publication Data
Frager, Dorothy.
    Cloth hats, bags 'n baggage.
    (Chilton's creative crafts series)
    1. Handbags. 2. Hats. 3. Luggage. I. Title.
TT667.F69   646.4'8   77-6116
ISBN 0-8019-6367-2
ISBN 0-8019-6368-0 pbk.

1 2 3 4 5 6 7 8 9 0   6 5 4 3 2 1 0 9 8

To my mother, Inez Lange, who taught me to sew,
and to all the creative women
who are willing to extend the needlecraft arts

Contents

Acknowledgments

Special thanks to my husband Victor, who supports all my creative efforts, and to my two sons James and Colin, who have become paragons of patience and delightfully creative, hard-working teenagers. I'm indebted to my exceptional aunt and uncle, Edith Heinrich for her constant encouragement and Kurt Heinrich for his ever-ready professional advice.

I wish to express my appreciation for the craft contributions made by Sonia Adams, Lorna Blauvelt, Mary Breitenbach, and Annelie Klienen, once students and now friends. Thanks for the unending patience of Harald Lindner of Target Photo, Inc., for the quality of the grouped color photographs and to Florance Treuer for her dependable typing. I am truly grateful to Marylou Hemingway, Julie Adams, Janet Gildred, along with my own family, for the modeling efforts.

Introduction

Welcome to the wonderful world of accessory designs! There are no new hat or bag designs in the world today—only new interpretations of old favorites.

Cloth Hats, Bags 'n Baggage was designed to extend the skills of hat and handbag making to a true creative craft experience. It is this utilitarian craft that has a delightful and unexploited artistic side. People express themselves each day with the selection of clothing worn. Why not make the two most useful accessory items into artistic garments for oneself, for a gift, for profitable sale items, for group participation, or for creative classroom projects. Each item selected to go into this book has current fashion appeal and is shown in several variations to help spark the imagination. The styles do not have to be highly fitted, a true blessing for the crafter. There is no limit to the combination of fabrics and trim to be used. It is a craft that can use skills already acquired, such as embroidery, applique, quilting, crewel, or even needlepoint. Initial cost of the projects is low and the time spent to produce an item can be as short or as extensive as one cares to devote. The work can be accomplished with machine techniques, by hand methods, or a combination.

Stylings were selected very carefully so as not to duplicate instructions, techniques, or trims. There are quick and easy styles to make, as well as highly decorative interpretations of challenging styles. Included are the tricks of the trade—how to make patterns, the standard techniques, the right vocabulary, and a good basic knowledge of the right fabrics and equipment. Techniques such as seam finishing and outside trimming are discussed in general and, although they are suggested for specific styling, it remains the crafter's joy to use them as one's imagination dictates. All styles shown in this book were created from easily obtainable fabrics in local shops. There are no boutique or designer cuts used, although this type of fabric would enhance some styles. All the trimmings and hardware used can be obtained in local shops, found in every town in the United States (*see* Sources of Supply).

The junior bag section will help the younger creative minds to get started in this field. It will instill a feeling of self-sufficiency and provide an opportunity to produce low-cost useful gifts, extra credit projects for school and youth groups. It will develop a sense of color and proportion and provide an outlet for product creativity.

To best use this book, browse through the photographs first. Read Chapter One to gain a basic vocabulary; learn about outer fabrics, interlinings, quilting, about patchwork and applique so popular today; learn to make patterns, figure yardage, how the straps that are common to all bags are made, and techniques for stylized seams. The next chapters are filled with fashionable projects. They start out with the easy projects first. If one technique is integrated into the construction of a second item, rather than repeat instructions already given, the text uses references to earlier text and figures. Since crafters are creative thinkers, variations are suggested in all possible areas. There is such a wide range of materials accessible to the crafter, getting started will pose no problem.

Directions are written in step-by-step fashion; read each step first and study the accompanying pictures. Proceed with the work in hand, rereading each sentence and stopping for a breath at every period!

Line drawings are coded: solid white indicates the outside fabric; the dotted portions show interlinings; small crosshatch and printed patterns show linings.

Fabric layouts are given for the bags that have many parts. The code for the layouts is: F—front; B—back; Sd—side; Bot—bottom; St—strap; Fl—flap; WP—wallet pocket. For the hats, the following code is used: Br—brim; C—crown. Two single lines close together indicate selvage; note text references to fold lines. The most stretch will be indicated with triple arrows at the end of one line. Fold lines used for reference will show as a line of dots. Quilting is shown as a line of dashes.

1

Materials and Techniques

WORKING WITH PATTERNS

Most patterns in this book are fairly easy to follow. The easy patterns can be worked on large ¼″ graph paper or brown wrapping paper. Most of the bags will have only rectangles and squares to contend with. A few of the bag patterns and most of the hat patterns have more complicated shapes and it is best to work on 1″ grid graph paper, 18″ x 22″ size, that can be purchased at any big stationery store. It is difficult to get the two sides of a pattern exactly alike. It is best to draw a line down the center of the paper and do all the figuring off to one side only, then fold the paper in half and cut out the whole pattern. Most strap measurements are given to coincide with the instructional strap methods suggested in Chapter Two, but you, the bag crafter, can change this to suit your taste.

Patterns may be enlarged or reduced very simply once the basic pattern is made. In most instances, it is best to add ½″ seam allowances to the shape of the bag, but if you care to work with ¼″ seam allowances or a zigzag foot, that's okay, too. Most hat patterns are even easier, using rectangles, circles, and shaded patterns given to scale where possible. The hats are best worked with ¼″ seam allowances. Press curved seams of hats open over a tailor's ham, or presser's mitt on the end of a sleeve board, or a towel rolled up tightly and pinned into a ball shape.

SELECTING FABRICS

Today in the retail fabric market there is an abundance of sturdy, smart, and fashion-right fabrics available to the accessory crafter. Shops catering to the dressmaking home sewer carry many suitable fabrics. Don't overlook your own supply of leftover yardage or the shops that sell slipcover and upholstery fabrics. Remnant table yardage is always a good buy for the accessory crafter. Sewing together bits and pieces of scrap fabric to form pretty patchwork patterns makes cost-saving, interesting, and unique items. An important cost-saving factor for making cloth hats and bags is that they can be made totally washable with most of today's fashion fabrics. Woollike fabrics are not always 100% wool and many are even washable. There is washable velvet out now. So learn the details of a fabric and have guarantees written on the sales receipt.

3

Characteristics and Suitability

JUDGING FABRICS

The fabrics you use should be fairly crush-resistant and tightly woven. Pull a few threads from the edge and, if you find that they come apart too easily, it may be assumed this will not wear well at the stress points of the bag (corners, openings and straps) or the hat (edge of the brim). Check on surface finishes. Most of the time, it will tell on the top of the bolt; if not, ask the salesperson.

All-cotton fabrics can be used with synthetic combinations if they are similar in weight. A poor match would be gingham with canvas; a good match would be broadcloth with pique and gingham or velvet with satin. Check for colorfastness and shrinkage at the point of purchase. It is best to use colorfast and preshrunk fabrics. You can preshrink many fabrics at home yourself if you are in doubt.

WASHABILITY

Today we are all "wash and wear" conscious. Accessories do get dirty and will need to be cleaned from time to time. If you would like to be able to wash your item, then concentrate on using only washable fabrics. There are many beautiful types that have a long life if cared for properly. If you choose to work with coatings, upholsteries, tapestries, and cut velvets, then you must have them dry cleaned. These have a long life, too, if cared for properly. If you are in doubt about their shrinkage, have them steamed by your dry cleaner first.

PRINTS AND STRIPES

On a relatively small item, such as an accessory, we want to get the optimum look from the patterns we are using. Measure the size of the pattern piece you are cutting. Measure the motif of the pattern in the fabric you are cutting. Make sure, if you are using only one pattern motif, that there is an even amount of background surrounding it.

Say you want to use a piece of slipcover fabric with a woodland duck printed every so often, for the flap and back of a bag. On almost every flap there is a portion that bends from the back over the top opening, then falls down the front of a bag. Well, the duck must fit the portion of the flap that falls over the front or else the head may be lost over the top of the bag. The viewer of the bag will be looking at a headless duck.

If you really want to use a print with a single motif and you discover it is too big to fit with the proper amount of background, make the bag larger. The background material will act as a frame for the single motif. Remember to add the seam allowance when you measure.

A good trick to accentuate a single motif is to pad only the motif with extra layers of batting. Place this over the interlining and then quilt around the motif.

Stripes can be worked in many ways. The stripes on a flap back and front may run in a head-to-toe direction, but the sides and straps can run horizontally. An even stripe may be chevroned on the flap by cutting the flap pattern in half, adding a seam allowance, then placing each half on the diagonal across the bias grain of the fabric. Sew stripes, creating a chevron at the center seam.

When working with an all-over pattern of smaller motifs, make sure that the highlights will not be covered by the straps. In general, smaller prints with good color contrast to the background are best, whether they are chintz florals or art nouveau geometric effects. Stripes are good for bags but very hard to work with for hats. Half-inch and under stripes are better than wider ones. Many times, in working with print materials—whether printed or woven designs—you may need a little extra so that you can place paper patterns on the fabric to take advantage of the best display of prints.

Daytime Bags and Hats

These are the items in your wardrobe that get the most use and abuse, whether on the way to work, the grocery store, or to and from the classroom. Fashion dictates a casual manner of dress for today's women and this is reflected in the accessories we wear. Hats and bags are accessory items that can be highly decorative and, if you like, a little on the wild side.

Woven fabrics, as opposed to the vast variety of knits, are best for a daytime handbag. If you are not sure what a knit looks like, examine the back; it will resemble the inside of your hosiery. If you are still uncertain, then ask the shopkeeper. In general, knits should be avoided; they are very stretchy and the fine surface yarns will be pulled with the hard wear that a daytime bag gets. However, they are ideal and even essential for many hats that are fashionable today.

The best woven fabrics are those used to make sportswear, such as jackets, skirts, and pants. *Gabardine* is a tightly woven twill weave that is easy to identify by its fine surface of tiny diagonal ribs. *Denim*, another superior twill weave fabric, is available in the plain blue-jean look or with a brushed, embroidered, or interestingly dyed surface. From the plain weave family, you can use fabrics such as heavy *poplin, duck, linen, sailcloth,* and *canvas.*

Another popular friend of the home sewer is the large family of *corduroys*, from the pinwale weight used in children's clothing, to the novelty high and low wale combinations, to the brushed surfaces new in today's pants market. *Drapery* fabric of a casual nature is another good buy, either in all cotton or a cotton and linen combination. Good old pillow *ticking* is readily available and its favorite form is the traditional woven stripe. The new *suede cloths* look just like the real thing and are washable. Some have a suede finish on both sides, some on only one side. There are also some *tapestries* and *upholsteries* available to the retail market, but most must be dry cleaned.

There are wonderful, lightweight fabrics that can be used successfully if handled correctly. These are the fabrics that are used for summer dresses and blouses. *Gingham, pique, poplin, broadcloth, seersucker, percale, madras, challis,* and *shantung* are good examples. They come in solid colors and in prints that range from old-fashioned calicos to modern geometrics. These thinner fabrics need strong interlinings behind them to give them support and they will work superbly when quilted, too. There are many prequilted fabrics available in the sewing shops today. These fabrics are quilted very well for clothing, but this stitching is not strong enough for accessories. The stitches quickly come out with wear but can be reinforced by requilting the original to the interlining.

FABULOUS FAKES

With the emergence of fake furs into the home sewing market, women are discovering the fun of using this stunning high-fashion fabric for accessories. When used properly, any fake fur can be an eye-stopping accessory, adding a quiet, elegant smartness to any costume.

The hardest part of working with fake fur is choosing a good one. Start with a reputable shop. Most fake furs are 54″ to 60″ wide. Backings may be woven or knitted and of cotton or synthetic fibers. The face is called the pile. It may be made of polyester, acrylic, modacrylic, rayon, or wool. There are very few of these fakes that are washable, so check the cleaning instructions. The pile generally runs in one direction. Check the entire piece you are purchasing to make sure the pile all runs in the same direction. The fashion emphasis on different fur types will change with the whims of fashion, but cutting particular furs in the right direction will always be the same. Smooth, sleek, short-haired furs (leopard) run downward. Long-haired furs (fox) run downward. Curly furs (Persian lamb) have no direction. The accessories designed here have taken into consideration the pile direction; to supersede this, we have worked out designs that use chain and novelty rings in the handle area. General layout and cutting information should be adhered to carefully.

Prewash all *washable* fur fabrics to prevent shrinkage later. At the edge of the fabric, mark the direction of the fur on the wrong side. Make patterns and mark the direction of the fur as indicated in the patterns given. If the fur has stripes, place the first pattern piece (generally the front piece) on the fur on the wrong side, checking through on the right side to take advantage of the stripe designs. The stripe on the back and side pattern pieces will have to match the stripe on the front. The trick to this is to stick a few pins from the front through the back, indicating where the stripes appear. With a pencil and ruler, draw the lines on the back of the fur and withdraw the pins. Attach pattern to the wrong side with as few pins as possible, placing the pins through the fabric backing only. An alternate method would be to draw the pattern pieces directly on the fabric back. Cut with the tip of very sharp shears, cutting through the backing only. Turn each piece to the right side and clip the pile from the seam allowance. Use your vacuum to clean up.

Use heavy-duty thread, a number 15 to 18 sewing machine needle, regular or zipper foot, and 10 to 12 stitches to the inch. Check the machine instruction book under heavyweight fabrics for tension adjustments. Using scrap, make some test seams. Place the basting pins in the fabric across the seam line at right angles, and stitch in the same direction as the pile. When stitching long-pile furs, be sure to smooth the pile away from the seam allowance before stitching. When sewing by hand, use a double length of thread and a backstitch. Some of the pile will be caught in the seam on the outside. With the eye end of a long needle, raise the fibers caught in the newly made seam. On the wrong side, notch any curves and trim out any seams that are bulky. To open and flatten seams, hold steam iron 2″ above fabric and spray. While still damp, flatten with finger pressing. If you keep seam allowance to ¼″, opening the seam will not be necessary.

Afternoon Bags and Hats

Afternoon stylings will be made of the richer, dressier fabrics that may go to work but would not go to the supermarket or to school. Suitable heavyweights would include the family of fabrics called *coatings: chinchilla, Ottoman faille, duvetyn, zibeline, fleece, wool gabardine,* and *tapestries.*

The medium weights are called "dress or costume" yardage: *wool crepe, flannel,* plain and printed *wool broadcloth,* printed *wool challis,* and, the one exception to the general ban on knit fabrics for handbags, the *double-faced wool knit.* The entire family of *velvets* are good buys. *Cut velvet,* sometimes found in the dress yard-goods shop or in upholstery yard-goods departments, is a better buy for the bags discussed in this book than a true velvet. The cut velvet has a design raised above a base of satin or flat weave. It looks as if the background has been cut away, leaving only a raised velvet design.

Evening Bags and Hats

Evening bags are just smaller versions of large bags, made in glamorous fabrics with delicate trimmings. Evening hats are the same as daytimers, but take on a magic effect made in dressy fabrics. Fabric is not chosen for its durability, but rather for its effect. Trimmings are added for a touch of elegance. Think of designing another jewel for the costume, rather than something to carry your paraphernalia in or to keep you warm.

There are four really big fabrics for the after-hours bag: satin, crepe, brocade, and velvet. These are the old dependables that go with almost anything and are generally easy to work with. *Satin* is a smooth-surfaced fabric with long floats that give a lustrous effect. All colors are stunning, but only black, white, red, and emerald green are easy to match with a wide variety of trimming, such as braids, frogs, or fringes. The heaviest weight satin made of synthetic blends is preferable, because most often a spot can be sponged out. *Crepe* has a textured surface which is achieved by crimping or twisting the yarn before weaving. It has a dull surface and a very soft hand (meaning soft to the touch). Lightweight crepe is particularly good for gathered hats and bags and heavyweight crepe is good for a highly shaped styling. Crepe is also used as a lining for late-day bags of other fabrics.

Brocade is a fabric woven on a jacquard loom, with raised and lowered surface yarns creating a continuous pattern repeat. This is used mostly to make fabrics of all gold and silver, or the metallic yarns are used in contrast with satin or twill weave ground. *Damask* is a cousin to brocade but is reversible, generally made with glossy and dull yarns to the design.

Velvet is a lustrous short-pile fabric now made in synthetic fibers. The denser the pile and heavier the backing, the more valuable the velvet for accessories. Sometimes the pile is heat pressed to give a crushed look. This comes and goes in the fashion picture, but it makes a very serviceable bag or hat. The closest cousin is *velveteen*, an all-cotton fabric with a dull surface and a shorter pile. Another member of the velvet family is cut velvet, described earlier. For very dressy, luggage-type bags, cut velvets made in upholstery weights are smashing!

For the evening bag, the entire family of *knit* fabrics can be used. They range from sheer prints, with metallic yarns traced delicately to enhance the prints, to soft-as-silk acetate and matte jerseys, to stretchy knit metallics, to beautiful soft-textured wool types.

Other good selections flattering to late-day styles are bengaline, faille, challis and foulard. *Bengaline* is noted for its finely woven cross-ribs and looks like grosgrain ribbon. With its dull finish, it makes up beautifully in firm styles. Its close cousin is *faille*, a lighter weight material best used in the gathered styles. Often *moire* effects are heat pressed onto a lightweight faille, giving it a water-stained appearance. *Challis* is most often found in wool or cotton and is a lightweight fabric, typically with Persian or Indian prints. For late day it is eye-catching and sequins and beads can be added to further enhance the prints for evening. *Foulard* is a twill weave fabric, originally made and used mostly for men's ties, but now available in synthetic blends with cravat or all-over paisley prints.

Tapestries were originally hand-woven fabrics; they are now simulated by machine, generally with a pattern of a geometric or pictorial nature. They are to be found in both home sewing shops and upholstery shops. Look for sharp contrast of colors. *Velour* in the home sewing market is a synthetic knit-base fabric that has a brushed surface. It has a plush look and comes in a marvelous range of colors, very suitable for accessories.

There is an entire family of sheer fabrics, often left over from dress yardage, from which a matching bag or hat could be made. They do best in the gathered styles. The most interesting gossamer effects can be had with *chiffon, lace, netting, tulle, marquisett, organza,* and other open, novelty weave fabrics. These materials are hard to cut and often slip and slide, so spread an old bedsheet on the cutting surface to help stabilize the fabric. Often it can be pinned inside the cutting line to the bedsheet, then cut very carefully with long strokes of the scissors. Each one of these see-through fabrics must have a second fabric underneath it. Handle both fabrics as one, basting them together. It will create an illusion.

Interlinings

FOR BAGS

This is the part that gives a handbag a long life. It is the signally most important part of the bag. If made properly, the outside fabric will be handled as one with the interlining, which will support the outer fabric and maintain the shape of the bag. Because it serves as a framework for the bag, the interlining must be of the highest quality. The traditional fabric for interlining washable bags is called *drill*. This is an off-white, heavyweight twill weave fabric 30″ to 32″ wide and generally made of cotton. It is not to be confused with cotton duck, which comes in pretty colors at 45″ wide and is used for sportswear. There are very few substitutes for drill. Some might include real pillow ticking, real pants denim, or canvas, but these are all more expensive. If your local retail shops do not carry drill, look in the telephone directory for trimming supplies stores or try the large mail-order catalogue stores. But do not let anyone tell you it's not made anymore (see Sources of Supply). The regular interlinings sold for making clothing are not strong enough. So search out a most sturdy interlining, or all the quality of the outside materials and trim will be lost after a few weeks of wear.

The second interlining used in bags in this book is Permette, made by Conso Corporation. It is used in the envelope styling only and is discussed there. It is purchased in drapery supply departments.

For straps, it is best to use *washable* belt interlining. It looks like screening and is sold in 1″ to 3″ widths, by the yard. There are nonwashable belt interlinings, too. These can be used if the bag is going to be dry cleaned. The strap must hold its shape, as it is both a heavy wear point and a very visual point.

FOR HATS

This is easy to come by in any dress goods shop. Take the fabric chosen for the outside of the hat and place it over the interlining to feel its weight. There are nonwoven interlinings with no grain to worry about. Note that these come in several weights. If making the velvet cloche, the heavyweight is preferred, as opposed to the same hat made in blended cotton gingham checks for a golf hat. In this case, the lightweight would be preferable. There are many woven interfacings. The best to start off with is Sari, a medium weight used mostly to interline blouses.

Linings

The attractive inside of a bag or hat is the lining. It serves to cover all the seams and generally adds to the decoration. The manufacturer of accessories will always seek to cut costs and use the most economical material here, because it is the outside of the bag that has the most appeal at the point of sale. For the crafter, this need not be so. The inside can be just as cheerful as the outside.

FOR HANDBAGS

The fabrics to look for are good cotton or cotton and synthetic blends that are opaque. *Broadcloth, gingham, sateen, pique, seersucker,* and *poplin* are good examples. These are fabrics that might also be used for outer wear.

FOR HATS

It may be a good idea to ask the shopkeeper to show you lining fabric. He will probably show you linings used in dressmaking, such as *taffeta, lawn,* or *batiste*. Make sure they are relatively opaque. Add to your list lightweight *satin, crepe, foulard, surah, china silk, nylon tricot,* and *Sibone.* The trick to selecting a lining for a hat is to place the outer fabric over the lining and interlining, if one is planned, to see if the firming effect or a soft draping effect is achieved. If working with a firm fabric, then the first six fabrics mentioned above would be good. If working with a soft draped look, then the last five would be good suggestions.

DECORATIVE TECHNIQUES

Patchwork

Patchwork is the piecing together of small but similarly shaped pieces of material to form one large piece of fabric. Sensational patchwork designs can be made from scraps. For hats with pieced crowns, two or more fabrics can be used. For handbags, larger designs of patches can be made. Sometimes beautiful leftover yardage from a dress or blouse will need just the addition of a quarter of a yard of new fabric to make a new and fresh-looking piece of patchwork.

Here are a few suggestions for some classic perfection in patchwork. Note first that most patchwork is assembled on the machine, using twelve plain stitches to the inch, or by hand, using a "sharp" needle and running stitch or backstitch. There are two ways to approach making patchwork for handbags or brimmed hats. The first is to make a piece of patchwork fabric equal to the size recommended in the yardage requirement and then lay out your pattern pieces. The second is to make each pattern piece out of paper, then cut out the interlining and, finally, make just enough patchwork to cover each piece of the interlining. Either way, the fabric of patches has its seams pressed open and it is placed over the interlining and basted to it.

Simple patchwork begins with making a pattern for each different shaped patch (Fig. 1–1). Each piece is planned with ¼" seam allowances. Copy the pattern carefully onto cardboard. Cut the pattern out to look like a picture frame, indicating both cutting line (outside of pattern) and seam line (inside of pattern) with pencil on the back of the fabric, because stitching takes place on the back. Begin by sewing long strips of patches together horizontally. Next sew the strips together vertically to form the entire piece that is needed.

Small hats use 1" to 1½" squares. For medium-size handbags, use 2" squares and, for large handbags, use 3" size. You can use a 3" equilateral triangle and a slim-looking diamond shape in place of the square. Another good pattern to work out is a brick pattern, which is really a rectangle. As you know, bricks can be laid in so many varying patterns. With a small 1" by 2" or 2" by 3" rectangle, many of the brick patterns can be duplicated (Fig. 1–2).

Let us not forget the simplicity of the stripe. Made in many delicious colors, it can look like a parfait or smart geometric (see color section, Fig. 10). Experiment, combining squares and rectangles of different dimensions into a pleasing design.

Quilting

The word *quilting* refers to the stitches placed through two pieces of fabric that have a lightweight filler sandwiched between. The stitching then makes two weak fabrics into a strong, serviceable fabric (Fig. 1–2). It is used in handbag making to attach the outside fabric of the bag to the interlining, creating a strong bond. In hat making, it is used to stiffen or firm up a brim. The stitching goes through the outer fabric, interlining, and lining (often the same fabric as the outside of the hat). The stitching can easily be ac-

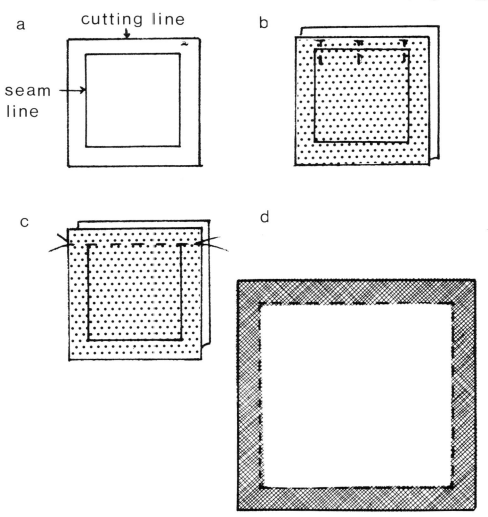

Fig. 1–1 Patchwork a. Cut template as you would a picture frame. b. Pin two pieces together, right sides facing. c. Stitch two pieces together (separately). d. Small pattern for template.

complished on the machine, using a medium-size needle, cotton or cotton-covered polyester thread, and a gauge of twelve stitches to the inch. It also may be worked by hand, using a hand sewing needle marked "between" size number 6 or 7 and quilting thread.

The softest filler is called batting and is used in handbag making. It helps to accent the quilt stitching and create an interesting surface texture on the fabric. The best battings are the polyester or cotton varieties used for blanket quilting. They are readily available in the retail stores and mail-order catalogues. This batting can be bought in small crib-size sheets, measuring 45″ by 60″, or full blanket sizes for many projects. You will cut the batting ½″ smaller all the way around than the outer fabric and the interlining, unless advised differently in the instructions. The batting is placed between each piece of outer fabric and interlining, creating a sandwich effect, then basted and quilted before final assembly of an article.

A plain solid color can have interesting stitchery designs made with contrasting color

Fig. 1–2   Suggestions for quilting stitches and patterns.

thread and plain running stitch or decorative machine stitches. Always start quilt stitching from the center of each piece, working toward the seam allowance.

One successful type of quilt stitching is the diamond pattern (Fig. 1–3). It is easily worked by placing the unit to be quilted in front of you on the work surface, outer fabric face up, batting next, with the interlining on the bottom. Find the true bias by folding the top of the fabric to meet the side, then press (Fig. 1–4). Fold in the opposite direction to form an X across the work. Place the first lines of quilting on the right side, duplicating the two fold lines and allowing the stitches to run to the edge of the triple-layered unit. Turn work to the back and, with a pencil and a ruler, mark off the successive lines to be quilted (stitching 1″ to 1½″ apart is good for handbags). Stitch along the freshly drawn lines on the wrong side of the fabric. The diagonal lines will cross each other, forming a diamond pattern. The squares of patchwork can have the quilting placed on the diagonal, crossing the squares, forming big Xs through each square.

Machine quilting can also be done with zigzag attachments. A wide-open type of zig-zag, feather, or ball stitch can be placed over the seam line. The thread can match or it may be used to create an accent. Try the stitches on your machine on a sample and check the needle size and thread tension suggested in your own machine instruction book. Try for a very unique look. Don't be afraid to let your imagination work for you. That's what all designers in the clothing business get paid for. Pattern designs, such as florals, geometrics, or other novelty effects, can be quilted (Fig. 1–5). To enlarge the amount of quilt stitching, go around the original line of stitchery about ¼″ to ½″ on the outside of the first line, using the presser foot as a guide. When using many such lines, this is called concentric line quilting. This is done also to accent an applique or stiffen a brim on a hat.

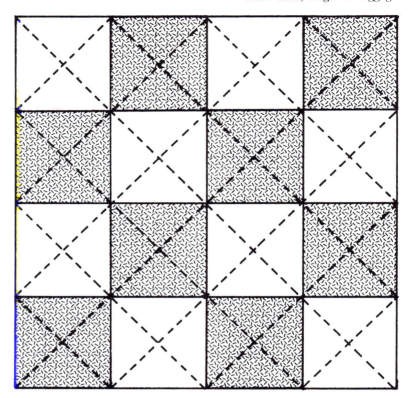

Fig. 1–3 Closeup
of diamond pattern
quilting.

The use of batting can be twofold. One, it serves to insulate, and two, it helps the stitches create a depression on the upper fabric, thus giving a textured look to the surface. Batting can be eliminated and quilting applied to surface fabric against the interlining. Do this when the outer fabric is already heavy and the quilt stitchery will be used to help shape or to help create additional design. Dressmaker's silk buttonhole thread will add an interesting touch to a dull surface. A little experimenting is needed to find the right quilted look for each fabric. (See color photos of patchwork hats and bags.)

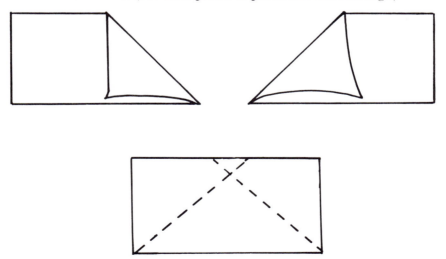

Fig. 1–4 Finding the true bias for diagonal line or diamond pattern quilting.

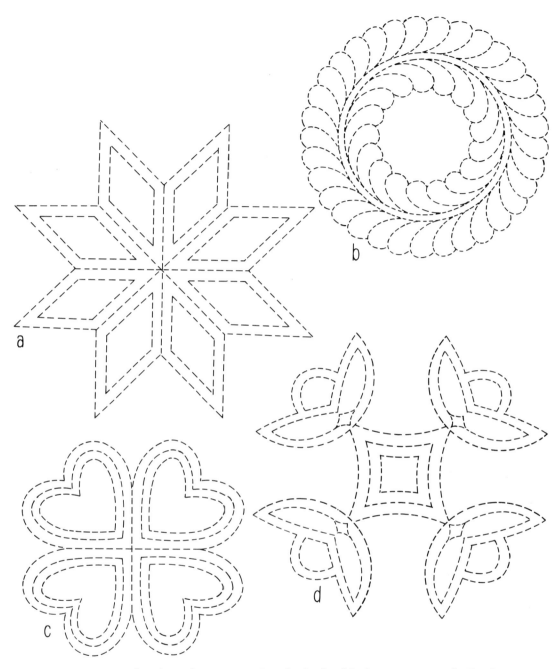

Fig. 1–5 Assorted quilt stitch patterns a. Star. b. Circle of feathers. c. Hearts. d. Floral.

Applique

The art of applying a small piece of fabric to a background fabric, creating a pictorial decoration, such as a flower or an animal, is applique. While it can become quite an accomplished art, it behooves the crafter to keep to simple subjects and a firm stitch to attach the selected material to the background. Appliques are generally applied only to the

Fig. 1–6   Folded-back edge of applique
with curves clipped.

flap of a handbag as decoration (see color section, Fig. 6). They may also be applied to
both brim and crown of a hat (see color Fig. 10).

Any one or a number of figures can be cut and applied. Patterns can be worked out,
using simple shapes copied from newspapers, children's coloring books, or juvenile picture books found in the library, or simply by looking at nature and interpreting its forms,
such as a star, a leaf, or a daisy. Draw an exact outline on the face of the fabric to be cut
out, then add $1/4''$ seam allowance beyond that and cut out on that line. Clip all curves $1/8''$

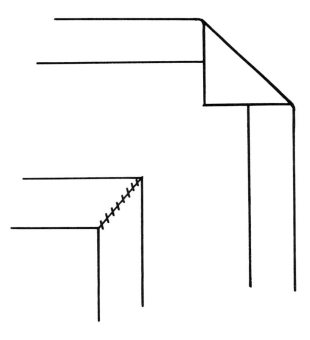

Fig. 1–7   Mitering excess fabric from a corner by first folding
the corner point to the inside,
then turning the side seam allowances toward inside. Finish
with small stitches. Baste all
edges.

Fig. 1–8   Three-piece Farm Boy applique, showing first row of basting in light-colored thread, second row of basting stitches attaching applique to background in dark thread, ready for final applique stitching. The small fabric shirt oval is placed against the background first. Then the overalls are placed on top and the hat last, overlapping top of shirt and overalls.

deep and slash into inside corners the depth of the seam allowance (Fig. 1–6). Turn and baste the 1/4″ seam allowance to the wrong side, mitering all corners and points (Fig. 1–7). Baste into position on the hat or bag (Figs. 1–8 and 1–9). For handbags, apply the applique before assembling; for hats, the sequence is optional.

Choose one of the following stitches to secure the applique. By hand, use a "sharp" needle and regular thread with running, overcast, blind, or buttonhole stitch. With the machine, use a straight running stitch or any of the fancy zigzag embroidery stitches. The hidden slipstitch is the most artistic of all. It is made by tunneling the thread through the

Fig. 1–9   Closeup of applique and quilting of handbag and flap.

edge of the applique a tiny distance, coming out and making a tiny stitch in the back (Fig. 1–10). The stitch goes particularly fast if you can pick up the work in your hand. Fold the backing material back against itself to form two folded edges. Then you will see yourself slipping in and out of each folded edge, one stitch slipping through the applique, the other through the background. The real trick to this is a *short* needle marked *sharp*.

Hand embroidery stitches can be used at any time on hat and handbag creations. Make sure the yarns you are embroidering with are washable if the finished item is to be washable. The brim of a hat and the flap of a handbag are the two prime targets to show off needlework. It would be wise to baste the interlining to the wrong side of the outside fabric and embroider through both. The lining will cover the back side of your stitching. See Fig. 1–11 for a few embroidery ideas.

Monograms

A personal touch needed so much in fashion today can be achieved with monogramming. It also helps to quickly identify luggage when traveling.

Fig. 1–12 shows several variations you might try. Block letters are the boldest and easiest to draw, using a ruler and graph paper. Arrange the letters in a vertical or horizontal design. Felt is quick to cut out and stitch, but iron-on patch material is even faster. Delicate script letters can be embroidered onto the background in cotton or crewel wool yarn. Although the embroidery is beautiful, it is time consuming.

Fig. 1–10   Closeup of hidden slipstitch.

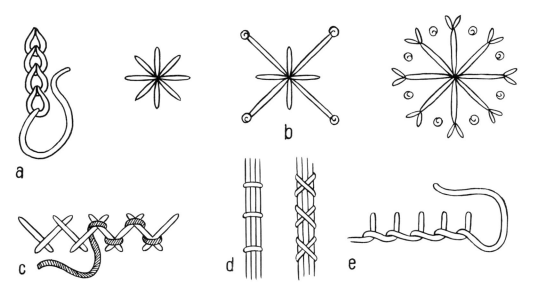

Fig. 1–11   Embroidery stitches a. Chain stitch. b. Stars of straight stitches. c. Herringbone interlaced with a contrasting color. d. Couching. e. Buttonhole stitch.

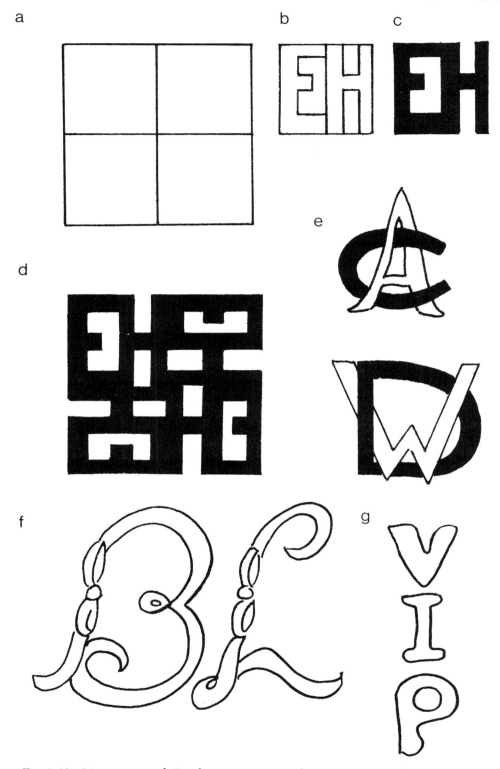

Fig. 1–12 Monograms. a–d: Two-letter monogram in box. e–g: Suggested lettering styles.

One of the most novel of all treatments, which combines monogramming with a spark of imagination, is the monogram whirling around in a square box (see Fig. 1–12*a* to *d*). You will need an 8″ x 12″ square of graph paper and an 8″ x 8″ piece of felt. Begin by making the monogram: On 1″-grid graph paper, draw an 8″ x 8″ square and divide in half vertically and horizontally to form four 4″ x 4″ squares (Fig. 1–12*a*). Beside this, on the graph paper, draw a second square 4″ x 4″ and divide this square vertically in the center. Place each of two initials in each rectangle, using block letters. Make the letters join or touch each other across the center line (Fig. 1–12*b* and *c*). Cut the letters out so that you have one two-letter monogram pattern and retrace four times into the four squares of the large monogram box. See Fig. 1–12*d* for the direction of the letters. For accuracy, shade the letters on the paper with darker marker and cut out the unused background. Use this as a pattern for contrasting color fabric. Press flat after cutting, then applique or iron on with some of the new fusing materials. This is excellent for tailored handbags and luggage.

FINISHING SEAMS

Piping

Cording, welting, and piping are all the same thing, but piping is the most popular term used. *Piping* is the encasing of a cord yarn in a bias strip of fabric. It is used as a surface decoration in the seam line. *Cording yarn* is loosely twisted cotton that is purchased by the yard in many thicknesses. Cut a bias strip wide enough to go around the cording yarn, plus a ½″ seam allowance for either side. The cording is centered against the wrong side of the bias fabric and the fabric is folded in half, covering cording yarn. Using small stitches, place the zipper foot on top of the fabric against the cording yarn bulk, stretching the fabric slightly. Do not stitch so closely that the cord is trapped tightly in the tubing (Fig. 1–13).

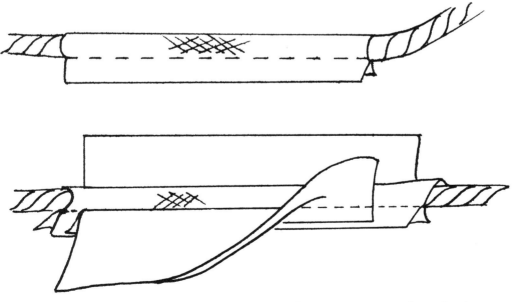

Fig. 1–13   (*Top*) folding the bias tape over the cording; (*bottom*) setting premade cording between two pieces of fabric.

Premade piping may be purchased in the store in standard colors. It looks as if it has a knitted material over the cord and only has one seam allowance. It is used on tailored dresses and suits. Welting is a piping, too, but it is covered with a twill weave material and is used in the seams of slipcovers and upholstery. It is sold by the yard in shops that sell slipcover material and it is keyed to the popular colors in home fashions. Piping and cording can be found very small, to be used only on hats and evening bags. Packages can be purchased at most notions counters in standard colors only.

To apply piping, place it against the right side of one of the pieces (front of bag or lower edge of flap along the seam line), with seam allowance of the piping laying over seam allowance of the piece it is to be applied to (Fig. 1–13). The stitches holding the cording yarn into the bias strip will be placed exactly along the seam line of the unfinished edge. Stitch by machine, running the *zipper* foot close to the bulk of the covered cording yarn, as shown. Hand baste the second piece over the first piece, matching raw edges of the seam allowances. Turn the work to the side that shows the first row of machine stitches and sew the two units together with the cording between, keeping the permanent stitches closer to the bulk of the cording tape than original stitches. This turning of work on the side showing the original line of stitches is the trick of getting a tight seam on the cording. The piping-cording technique should be used when additional surface decorations are needed or when additional stiffening is needed around the perimeter of the bag, as on the flap or the outside seams. This is not a beginner's technique. (See color, Fig. 5.)

Double-Fold Braids

This material is of a woven bias construction so that it can be easily shaped around flat and curved edges. It is used in the handbag craft to cover seams that have been turned to the outside. It serves two purposes: first, it adds a decorative feature to the outside of the bag; secondly, by turning the seams to the outside and covering them with braid, no lining is needed in the bag (see the canvas totes and the spacemate hanging garment bags.)

The braid is prefolded and comes in several textures. The polyester material looks

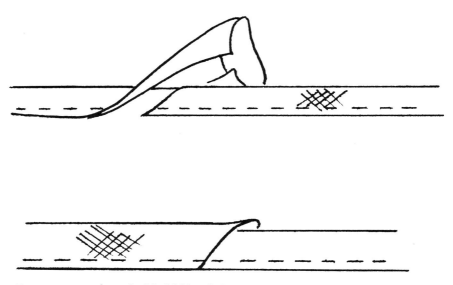

Fig. 1–14   Finishing double-fold braids by overlapping raw ends on the diagonal.

like cotton, but is very smooth. The cotton material is soft and dull and can stand the most abuse, while the most glamorous member of the double-fold braid family is made with a shiny synthetic yarn and is used on dress bags only. All the materials are made in many colors, from the lightest to the darkest shades.

It is a good idea to baste the seam together, then slip the double-fold braid over the raw edge, covering the basting stitches. Stretch the folded edge to fit around the outward curves and baste, then topstitch in matching color thread, sewing through both sides with one row of stitches 1/8″ off the edge of the braid (Fig. 1–14). If the bag is large, a second row of stitches can be added for additional strength. If the ends are to be joined, such as in the spacemate garment bags, then fold back one end and lap it over the other raw end on the diagonal for best results (Fig. 1–14). This diagonal fold eliminates bulk. If the bag is to receive a great deal of wear, then hand stitch the remainder of the diagonal fold to secure it and prevent fraying.

Double Topstitch and Raised-Edge Seams

These seams decorate and strengthen at the same time. The thread makes a definite statement, so make sure you use heavy duty or glossy thread.

The double topstitch seam is now used in the manufacture of upholstered furniture in place of a welted edge on the soft pillows. It's a smart-looking seam for both bags and hats when handled right. Press a 1/2″ seam allowance open. Place a row of stitching 1/4″ to 1/3″ on either side of the seam line (Fig. 1–15). If you have a zigzag machine with fancy stitches, see how the various stitches will look in place of the plain machine stitch.

The raised-edge seam is used on very tailored bags to help give some rigidity to the shape. It is best to try to work this seam only on bags that have round corners, such as tote and luggage types. Begin by making a plain seam first. Working on the right side,

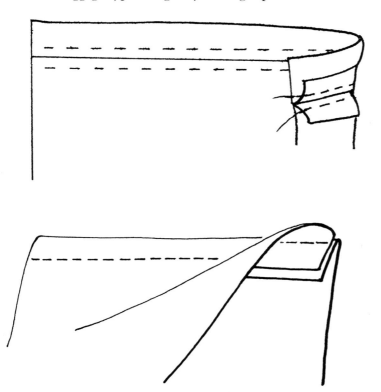

Fig. 1–15 (*Top*) double topstitch seam; (*bottom*) raised-edge seam.

crease along the stitched seam, placing the seam allowances together between the outer fabrics. Place pins at a 90° angle across the seam to hold it back. Begin stitching $1/8''$ off the edge with small stitches, using the zipper foot (Fig. 1–15). Completely encircle the outer shell of the bag. The remainder of the seam allowance on the inside of the bag may be trimmed slightly if it seems to be too bulky, and you may have to notch the corner seam allowance if you feel it is pulling.

2

Handbags

There are certain techniques specific to the handbag craft. As I said before, there are no new handbag designs, only new versions of old favorites. This comes from an intimate knowledge of the basic methods and technical points of making the various parts of the bag. Outlined here are suggestions for the most successful methods to make straps, private wallet pockets, and floorboards, and the imaginative use of hardware and closures. How you put these variables together with fabric and color determines whether the item is just a good, serviceable bag or a lively designer item.

STRAPS

Strap length is a matter of preference, depending on height and personal taste. At the present time, shoulder bags are in vogue. There are two lengths to consider. The regular shoulder length should place the main portion of the bag below the waist. The high shoulder seems to be preferred today. It would place the bag about 3″ below the armpit, with the bottom of the bag reaching the waist, or just below. The upper arm then can hug the bag, securing it tightly against the body and still allowing your hands to be free. The measurements given in this book are for average sized women. The tall and very short will have to make adjustments.

There are several methods of making straps—all are correct. If you find one method you like better than the others as you proceed to make each bag, then use it on all subsequent bags. The hallmark of a good-looking, long-wearing bag is a strap that keeps its shape and does not curl at the edges. Here is where lining the strap with a layer or two of washable belt lining really pays off. Additional lines of stitchery will strengthen and decorate the self-made strap.

There are sources of premade or partially made straps available to the home crafter, too. Start off by looking in the belt shop or your own closet. The soft crushed vinyl types are smart, as well as the narrow widths that may be braided or zigzag stitched together. In the craft supply stores, there is an abundance of rope and $1/4″$ leather lacing that is used for the art of macrame and could easily be fashioned into a braided strap. Crochet or knit a strap if you can and back it with belt interlining and grosgrain ribbon. Embroidered and grosgrain ribbons can be applied to daytime bags, while the velvets, satins, and metallic types combine best with late-day fabrics. All should have a supporting interlining and be lined. Filled tubing is great for day or evening. It is a bias or knitted narrow tubing about ¹/₄″ thick that has a cord pulled through its center. It is purchased by the yard and comes in fashion colors. It is very pliable and can be braided, knotted, or stitched together to form a strap. Don't forget metal chain, which is discussed under Hardware.

Self-Made Strap Techniques

Making a strap is a simple technique for the bag crafter. A few rules must be adhered to for a strong, serviceable strap. The strap must have some rigidity; to gain this, the crafter has to add an interlining that is very firm. The best material available today is a washable belt interfacing sold at all fabric shops. It looks like fine window screening. If it is not available in the width you require, then sew two narrower widths together, lapped over or zigzagged. A substitute for this material would be two pieces of drill or canvas interlining, folded in half and stitched together with lines set ¹/₄″ to ¹/₂″ apart.

There are two popular methods to put the straps together. Since the methods are explained here in detail, the instructions for each project will refer you to the method number.

METHOD ONE

This is called the two-piece strap. It has the distinct advantage of using a different color fabric on the lining side for decorative or economic reasons. Turn the two long seam allowance edges of the outside fabric (generally ¹/₄″ to ¹/₂″) to the wrong side and press. If batting is used, trim a piece to fit within the folded edges. On top is placed the interlining, trimmed to fit within the folded edges of the outside fabric.

Press the seam allowance on the two long edges of the strap lining to the wrong side and place it against the underside of the layered upper strap, wrong sides together. Baste to hold the edges even. Stitch by machine ¹/₄″ off the edge. For extra strength, place another row, or a few rows, of stitching within the first two (Fig. 2–1*a*). The more stitching, the stronger the strap. This is the method that would be used for a shaped strap or one planned with some sort of buckle.

METHOD TWO

This construction is what might be called a wraparound technique. The outside and its lining are made of one piece of the outside fabric, which is cut twice the width needed, plus ¹/₄″ for each seam allowance. This may be assembled in two ways. First, by centering the belt interlining against the center of the wrong side of the outer fabric (Fig. 2–1*b*). If a quilted strap is planned, then place a piece of batting the same size as the interlining under the interlining against the wrong side of the fabric. Fold one long side of the outer fabric over the interlining to the back, press, and baste close to the edge. Fold the seam allowance of the other long side to the wrong side, press and fold again, covering the raw edge already basted down. Baste this closed and then stitch permanently, as shown. If it is an evening bag, stitch by hand; if it is a daytime bag, stitch by machine.

Secondly, a variation of the same method may be used: Place one edge of the interfacing against the folds of the seam allowance, press the seam allowance over the interfacing, and baste (Fig. 2–1*c*). Fold the seam allowance of the other side of the strap to the wrong side, press and fold again in half, so that the newly folded seam allowance is placed against the first folded seam allowance. Stitch down by machine. Add a second row of stitches to match first on the opposite side. Add any decorative stitches that please you at this point.

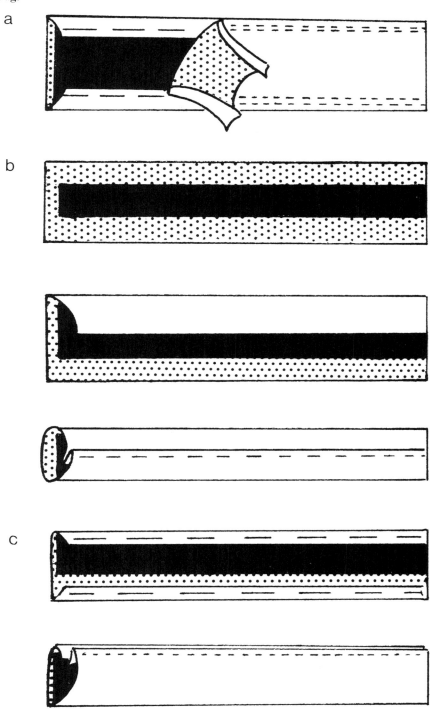

Fig. 2–1   Strap making a. Two-piece strap method. b. Centering interlining strap method: fold top to center; fold the bottom seam allowance to wrong side and fold bottom portion up to cover raw edge. c. Alternate strap method: Interlining placed under one seam allowance; bring the remaining side of strap over the seam allowance of top portion to cover interlining.

Luggage Webbing

There is a material available in some areas called *luggage webbing*. It generally is made of heavy cotton-type yarns, in 1″ to 2″ widths, usually in assorted multicolor stripes. Since it is woven, the design appears on the back. It can be used for handbag straps or belts. It needs no extra stiffening or lining material. When working with it, use *heavy-duty* thread and needle (see Fig. 2–6).

Double-End Snaplock Strap

This strap is simply a long piece of reinforced strap that has a snaplock attached to either end (available at hardware stores). When making a handbag, such as the envelope, or a piece of luggage, such as the duffle or the flight bag, insert small strong loop tabs at the sides where the strap will be attached. When a long strap is needed, snap on the longer strap, catching the snap locks in the loop tabs. It's another way of adding versatility to the craft item. The larger version is a harness latch (see Fig. 2–6).

LINING POCKETS

When designing a bag for specific use, it stands to reason that each of us carry some items of more importance than others. When planning a bag, items such as glasses, small change, important papers, and keys can be given a special pocket on the lining so they are easily found (Fig. 2–2). Pockets are sewn to the lining before linings are assembled.

Fig. 2–2   Pockets on the lining. All patch types, but the one in the middle is a loose wallet pocket, partially finished with double-fold braid.

Patch Pockets

The easiest type is called a *patch pocket* and it can be made of any fairly sturdy fabric. A patch pocket is made by cutting out a block of material, ¹/₂″ larger than needed on bottom and sides, and 1″ larger on the top. Turn the top back ¹/₂″ twice, concealing the raw edge. Press.

It may be permanently stitched back with a hemstitch or with the addition of rickrack, lace, or decorative stitchery in a contrasting color. Then press the ¹/₂″ seam allowance to the wrong side, mitering the corners. Place the wrong side of the pocket to the right side of the lining and topstitch sides and bottom before the bag is assembled. Either a straight machine stitch or a satin stitch on the zigzag machine can be used. Reinforce with a small triangle of stitches at top stress points (Fig. 2–3a).

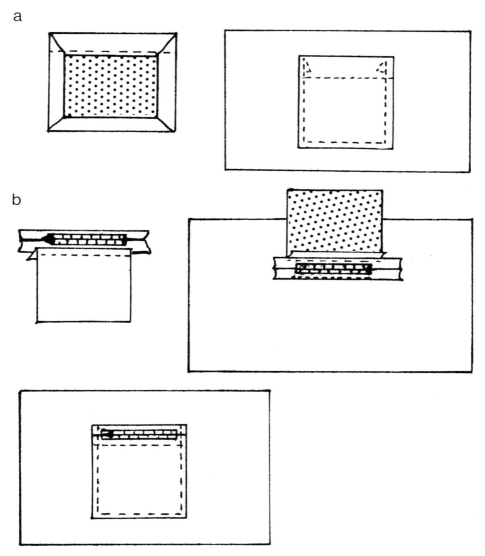

Fig. 2–3 Lining pockets a. (*Left*) wrong side of patch pocket; (*right*) right side: Reinforce corners. b. Steps for the quickie zip-top pocket: Attaching pocket to zipper; attaching upper portion of zipper to lining; attaching pocket to lining of bag.

Quickie Zip-Top Pocket

This pocket is attached to the lining before the bag is assembled, using the zipper foot on the machine. It requires only a 7″ to 10″ zipper, neckline or skirt type. Cut a piece of fabric 1″ wider than the length of the zipper. For example, if the zipper is 7″, cut fabric 8″ wide by 10″ deep. Pocket can be any depth that will be accommodated by the lining.

Working with the zipper closed, fold one 8″ side of the fabric to the wrong side 1/4″ and press. Topstitch the folded edge to one side of the zipper tape, placing the folded edge just below the teeth (Fig. 2–3*b*). Center pocket against the lining near the top of the bag in an upright position, right sides of fabric together, and stitch across the other side of the zipper tape. The stitches should be placed in the middle of the tape and begin and finish *three stitches beyond the ends of the teeth*, as shown. While it's in an upright position, fold the remaining 1/2″ edges of pocket sides and bottom toward the wrong side, ends of zipper tapes included. If tape ends are too long, trim to 1/2″. Press all the edges to hold in place. Turn down in right position, pin, and topstitch on all the edges 1/8″ off the sides and bottom and over the ends of the turned-in zipper tapes.

Private Wallet Pocket

This zipper-topped pocket will hold private papers and is a good idea to include in any bag that will be used for business or travel. The example given here will accommodate most bankbooks, checkbooks or passports. Materials: One 7″ zipper, either neckline (separating) or dress side opening type. Cut one piece of fabric 8″ wide by 16″ long. On both of the short 8″ ends of fabric, turn the raw edge to the wrong side 1/2″ and press. On the right side of the fabric, center and place one of the folded edges against one of the outside edges of the zipper tape, being careful not to cover the teeth of the zipper.

Stitch, using a straight running stitch and the zipper foot of the machine. Place the remaining folded edge against the other side of the zipper tape and stitch as above, being careful not to cover the zipper teeth. At completion you have a tube with a zipper in it (Fig. 2–4 *top*). Turn the tube to the wrong side and *open the zipper 1″*. Measure 1″ above the zipper and mark with a pencil line across the width of the fabric. Fold the tube lightly along this line to indicate this will be the top of the tube. Smooth out and fold lightly at the bottom, checking to see that raw edges are even (Fig. 2–4 *bottom*). Stitch the two sides closed, coming no closer than 1/4″ off the end of the zipper. Trim excess from tape ends to 1/4″ beyond the stitch line. Stick one finger through the opening in the zipper and open the zipper all the way. Turn the newly formed bag to the outside, close the zipper, and press. You now have a completely closed pocket. Place it against the bag lining and stitch 1/4″ off the edge on all four sides. For additional strength, add a second row of stitches across the top.

This technique may also be used to add an outside pocket onto a bag or a piece of nomad luggage. For a free-hanging wallet pocket, turn to instructions for canvas totes (see Fig. 4–3).

FLOORBOARDS

In manufactured bags, you find a hard bottom attached in some manner to the bottom of the bag to make it rigid. Most times this is placed between the lining and the wrong side of the outer fabric. It generally makes a bag impossible to launder because it's cardboard.

In this text I have been carefully striving to create bags that do not need the rigid bottom, but in some cases you may find it desirable. Many times quilting the bottom to a

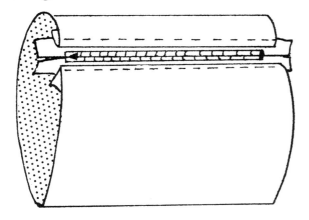

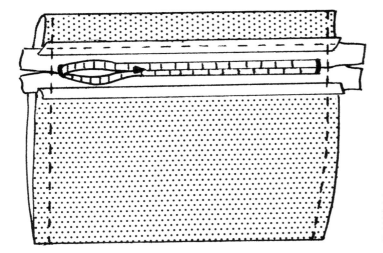

Fig. 2–4 Private wallet pocket: (*Top*) placing zipper in to create a tube; (*bottom*) stitching the sides.

firm interlining will do the job quite neatly, but to create a rigid bottom make a floor-board. This will require a piece of cardboard with pointed corners or a piece of very thin wood with filed-down corner points to fit the inside of the bag. This is covered with a small pillowlike casing of the lining fabric. Carefully draw the floorboard shape on scrap paper. Cut two pieces of fabric ½″ larger on the two long sides and one short side. Cut the remaining short side 1″ larger. This will be the open end, just as a pillowcase is made. Place the right sides of the fabric together. Stitch three sides with the ½″ seam allowance, backstitching to reinforce corners (Fig. 2–5). Clip corners and turn to outside, then press. Slip the rigid floorboard into the casing you have made. Turn the remaining raw edge to the inside, as close as possible to the narrow end of the floorboard. Stitch closed by hand or using a zipper foot on the machine (Fig. 2–5). When the washable bag needs laundering, open these few stitches, slip out the floorboard, and launder casing with the rest of the bag. Return the floorboard to its casing and restitch.

This board, having been covered with the lining fabric, is placed inside the already finished bag as a bottom flooring. This invisible flooring could be a good place to carry a little extra "mad money" when traveling. Floorboards can be decorative, with narrow lace or self-ruffled edges placed around the outer edges, or trimmed with scraps of colorful bias tape. The canvas bag project may need a floorboard. Wood can be obtained at the

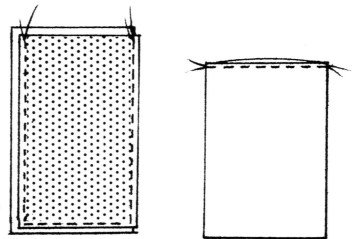

Fig. 2–5 Floorboards: (*Left*) making casing; (*right*) sewing up top.

lumberyard, hobby shop, or from supermarket fruit crates. (Note the thin strong board in a crate: The price is always right—free. Don't be afraid to ask, as these boxes are generally thrown out.)

HARDWARE AND CLOSURES

In the handbag industry, *hardware* includes the rigid frames, handles, closures, and rings that are generally of a decorative nature used to enhance the appearance of the bag. There are plenty of decorative options open to crafters (Fig. 2–6). At the top of the hardware resource list will be your trimming supply stores, followed by fabric shops, many of which have an ever-changing supply of belt and button items, and then there are your big hardware supply stores.

Start by asking for brass or metal rings, small, 1″ to 2″ decorative plaques, or small knobs of wood or metal. Look at the rigid key ring selection. There are rectangular spring-loaded key rings, novelty two-part rings and belt key rings with embossed leather tabs.

Try to avoid Saturday mornings when many other do-it-yourselfers are also seeking advice. If convenient, try late morning or early afternoon after professional tradesmen have gotten their supplies. I found some marvelous solid brass rings at a local store on a rainy afternoon when the shopkeeper had the time to think about my needs.

Chain

Hardware stores sell chain but most is too rough for handles. In some stores, colored plastic chain is available. Ask for silver basin chain. It looks like giant key ring chain and can be used for evening bag handles.

Drapery supply stores have marvelous chain for handles of bags—it is sold to use as tie-backs for draperies. It is smooth to the touch and comes in many widths and colors, shiny and antique brass, antique white, anodized silver, and dull black. Much of the chain used in the drapery market looks heavy and weighty, but is actually made of a material like aluminum and is very light. The evening bag of today sports a long shoulder-length chain on a tiny bag. This fine chain can be found at the jewelry counter of your local department store. Pet shops are another source for chain. You will, however, have to purchase it in leash lengths only.

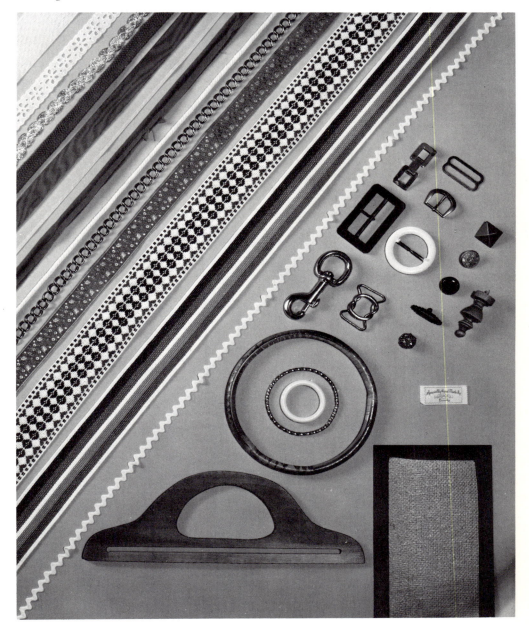

Fig. 2–6 (*From upper left corner*) washable belt interfacing, polyester eyelet, metallic novelty trim, double-fold braid, grosgrain ribbon, narrow soutache braid, piping, cording to put into piping, chain, French ribbon, embroidered cotton braid, luggage webbing, rickrack trim. (*From upper right*) buckles with and without shanks, including harness latch; assorted buttons—(*from top*) square, military, leather, toggle, rhinestone; one screw-in finial. (*Center*) assorted rings—large bamboo used for handles, gold twisted ring, opaque plastic ring. (*Bottom*) rigid wood handle for knitting bag; small label with personal name on it to be used for gifts; Permette on black paper background to set off the texture.

Buttons

Buttons are generally thought of as closures and in handbags they are used mostly with a loop-type button catch (see accordion bag). Buttons can set the tone of a bag, be it tailored or very feminine. Sparkly buttons, such as rhinestones, add a touch of elegance to the dark, simply made evening bag. Buttons can be placed at the bottom of a flap to look like a closure when actually they are only used for their decorative value.

Look for a short-shanked button, as the long shank may make the button look floppy when the bag is open. There are button departments in all major city department stores and many cities have individual button stores. Look in the phone directory—they are a joy to visit. Buttons can be found at antique and flea markets also, as they are collectibles.

Closures

The oldest closure is the good standard metal snap for the evening bag. You can purchase covered dressmaker snaps in standard colors—black, gray, and white. On a flapped bag, place the side of the snap with the "rounded prong head" on the flap side and the "depressed hole" side on the front of the bag. Anchor both into the interlining of the bag with heavy thread.

To replace the snapper, today's manufacturers have come up with a product called Velcro, made by Velcro Company. They have made this material into self-gripping fasteners shaped into small round dots that work much like snaps do, except they have tiny polyster "hooks" on one dot and nylon "loops" on the matchmate. They grip together amazingly and peel apart easily. To use on a flapped tote bag, stitch the "hook" side of the dot to the lower center of the flap lining before working the lining into the bag. After lining is sewn in permanently, use a hand stitch to attach same "hook" side dot to the interlining behind the lining. The "loop" portion will be stitched by hand or machine to the proper place on the front of the bag. This material works well as a closure.

Other closures include ready-made frogs. They come in standard colors—black, white, red, navy blue, gold, and silver. They are placed on the outside of the bag. These, too, can be made at home with a little practice, but only of thin materials. Small hooks and eyes are out of the question for handbags, but large, *covered* hooks and eyes are easily found in the trimming supply section in standard colors. They are placed under the flap in a hidden position. On the flapped bag, the "hook" would go on the flap and the "eye" on the bag, both being hand sewn and anchored to the interlining.

Zippers

The zippers best used for handbags are the metal zippers with large teeth and heavy woven side tapes. Ask for a separating zipper if possible, since it is the easiest to put into a handbag. It's the type put into the front of a sport jacket. The separating type generally provides the crafter with the opportunity to open the zipper and apply each seam tape into the front and back of the bag between the outer shell and the lining. The trick to accurate installation of this zipper is to place a small pencil dot on either side of the two top ends of the zipper tapes. This will serve as a point of reference when putting it into the bag.

Zippers come in standard sizes. Generally 12″ to 14″ length is a good size for handbags, but check the materials list carefully. If you wish to enlarge or reduce the bag pattern given, make sure you can get the zipper size you want. If the zipper is too long, then allow the additional amount to hang off the bottom end and, after all sewing is completed, close zipper, measure 1″ beyond the end of the bag, and cut through the tapes and between teeth. With a double length of thread, make six overcast stitches ½″ from the end or use your zigzag stitch on the sewing machine. Make a tab to cover the end of the zipper. Measure the width of the zipper and add $1/4''$ to the width measurement. Measure the length in the opposite direction, $1^1/4''$. Cut two pieces. Turn and baste the $1/4''$ edge all the way around on each piece. Place one piece under the tape end and one piece over the top of the tape end, covering the stitches and matching the edges of the two tab pieces. Stitch permanently with a row of top stitches around all four edges. If you have access to leather, than use the same process but without the seam allowances. This tab can be tucked down inside the bag or allowed to hang free.

Harness Snap Lock

This is the snap lock found most often at the end of a dog's leash, sometimes called a swivel-eye snap. It is a rigid ring that has a secondary spring loop clasp at the other end. It has been used on sporty handbags for many years. It is generally attached to a fabric band ($1''$ to $1^1/2''$ wide) that is attached to the back of the bag. This is then flipped over the top opening and brought down over the front so that the clasp can close over a ring of matching metal or a fabric loop attached to the front of the bag.

This type of closure can be found at pet, boating, or riding supply stores. The more decorative ones come in shiny metal finishes, such as chrome or brass, and sometimes the base metal is finished with an antique brass look. Be sure to get a matching ring. Since they come in several sizes, it would be a good idea to bring the finished outer shell of the bag to the shop and see how the various sizes look in relationship to the bag you are making. (*See* split-strap shoulder bag and Fig. 2–6.)

FIGURING YARDAGE

Yardage for handbags is very easy to figure out after you have made the initial paper pattern for the bag. Most of the pieces are square, rectangular, or derivative shapes. In this text, the selection of fabric and yardage is given for most obvious and accessible fabrics in the home sewing market. Yardage for most handbags is figured at 45″ wide, while fake furs are figured at 54″ to 60″ wide, because that is how fake furs are made. All the nomad luggage is based on canvas, which is 30″ to 32″ wide. It is the most accessible and logical fabric to use in learning how to make the heavy-duty bags.

If you wish to use a fabric width not suggested, such as a boutique import fabric or a remnant use the following technique for accurate results. On a large table work surface, piece together the width of fabric from old newspapers—about one yard long. Then begin to place the full-size pattern pieces. Bear in mind the best uses for the grain, keeping the strong lengthwise grain in a parallel position with the body. With a dark pen, mark the position of the pieces on the newspaper and proceed to use the newspaper as a buying or layout guide. Place pattern pieces on the fabric and cut carefully.

CLASSIC FLAP TOTE

This versatile tote is everyone's favorite. It was selected as the first bag because it is the one that has many easy parts for the newcomer to gain the best foundation in handbag crafting. It is shown in Fig. 2–7 with decorative quilt stitchery. You don't have to quilt this bag, but remember that its structure requires a strong outside fabric. The dramatic appeal of this bag is its flap decoration, which sets the tone (*see* color Fig. 6).

The rickrack and applique trims give the dark, serviceable bag a novelty look, and the applique floral motif immediately gives it a bold but feminine appeal. This bag could

Fig. 2–7   Classic flap tote: Note quilted detail on back and placement of rickrack trim tapes on flap.

be simply quilted in a contrasting color thread without additional decoration. Its overall size is 3″ x 10″ x 13″, with a 21″ strap.

MATERIALS

1 yard of 45″ outer fabric
1 yard of 45″ lining
1½ yards of 30″ interlining
45″ x 30″ piece of batting
two 30″ pieces of colored rickrack, optional
two pieces of small, contrasting color scraps (about 14″ x 14″, for applique)

PREPARATION

Using Fig. 2–8 as a guide, cut all the pieces given for the outside fabric, batting, interlining, and lining. Make a paper pattern first, using sizes given below, seam allowance included. Shape the flap as shown in layout, with shallow 1″ indentations just below its top; total length of the indented curve will be no more than 4″.

	Outer Fabric	Interlining	Batting	Lining
Front and back (14″ x 11″)	2	2	2	2
Side (4″ x 11″)	2	2	2	2
Bottom (4″ x 14″)	1	1	1	1
Flap (12″ x 13″)	1	1	1	1
Strap (4″ x 22″)	1 or 2	1	1	0 or 1

Seam allowances are planned for $1/2$″. The strap can be lined with the same material as the strap itself or with the lining fabric used for the bag. The dimensions given here are for a high shoulder bag; for a standard shoulder, make the strap longer.

ASSEMBLY

Step 1. Prepare the decoration on the front flap: all decorations should be no higher than 9″ from the bottom of the flap, because the other 4″ will form the top fold.

Rickrack Trim. Cut a large teardrop shape, approximately $6^1/2$″ by $4^1/2$″ (yellow). Turn back the edges $1/4$″. Applique the shape to the center of the flap 2″ from the bottom, using a hand whipstitch, a double length of thread, and a needle marked "sharp." Center a second, smaller teardrop, cut $4^1/2$″ by $2^1/2$″ (red), with its edges basted back $1/4$″ over the first applique. Using $1/2$″-wide rickrack (red), trim the largest teardrop shapes. Pin first, then secure each high and low point of the rickrack with hand stitches. Place a second row of rickrack (light blue) above the first, ringing the small teardrop. If any additional trim is desired for the outside of the bag, add it at this point to the outside pieces before they are assembled to the interlinings. Use Fig. 2–7 as a guide.

To follow the rickrack design shown in Fig. 2–7, place an additional length of red rickrack in a curved line approximately $1^1/2$″ above the bottom seam on the *front* piece of the bag. When the flap is closed, it will show below the curve of the flap. When the flap is open, it's just another decorative point of the bag. Allow all rickrack ends to run off the edges of the bag, and press.

Pink Floral Trim. Using opaque fabric, cut five (green) leaflets *t*, five (rose) petals *a*, and one (rose) center *c*, using the shapes in Fig. 2–9 as a guide. Add the $1/4$″ seam allowance to patterns given. Turn the $1/4$″ seam allowance to the back of the outer edges of the petals and top half of leaflets. Baste close to the edge. Place a fine row of hand gathering stitches across the base of all the petals and draw in gently, reducing each base to 1″. Arrange petals with leaflets peeking out from behind. Center on the right side of flap, mindful to stay at least $1/2$″ above seam allowance. Baste first, then secure with a hand blind stitch or small overcast stitch (Fig. 2–10). Place center circle, with seam allowance basted back, over the raw edges of gathered petals. Baste and stitch down with the very best stitches you can make. Press edges lightly. Do not crush the gathers.

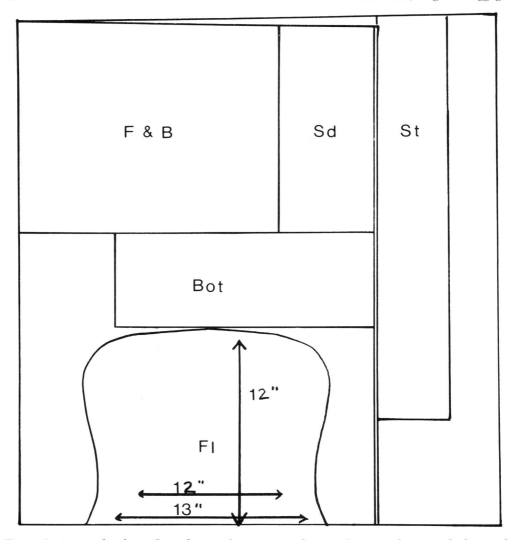

Fig. 2–8   Layout for classic flapped tote. There is unused material next to the strap if a lining of the same material is desired.

Assorted Color Trim. Plan for off-white muslin bag shown in color Fig. 10, with hat to match. Cut out eight assorted-color petals *d* and one dark center *c* (Fig. 2–9). Add the $1/4''$ seam allowance to pattern given. Turn and baste seam allowance to the back of each petal, mitering points (see Fig. 1–7). Place petals in a circle and baste to right side of the flap. Place center *c*, with its edges turned back, in the center. Baste and then stitch the entire flower down permanently.

Step 2. On the work surface, place the flap lining and the decorated flap with the right sides together. On top of this, place the batting and then the interlining. Make sure the edges are even and baste with a large X pattern; then baste around the raw edges.

Step 3. Stitch around the two sides and the bottom of the flap with $1/2''$ seams, catching all four layers. Trim interfacing and batting to $1/8''$ and clip notches at points of greatest curvature on seam allowances. Turn right-side-out so the lining is covering the

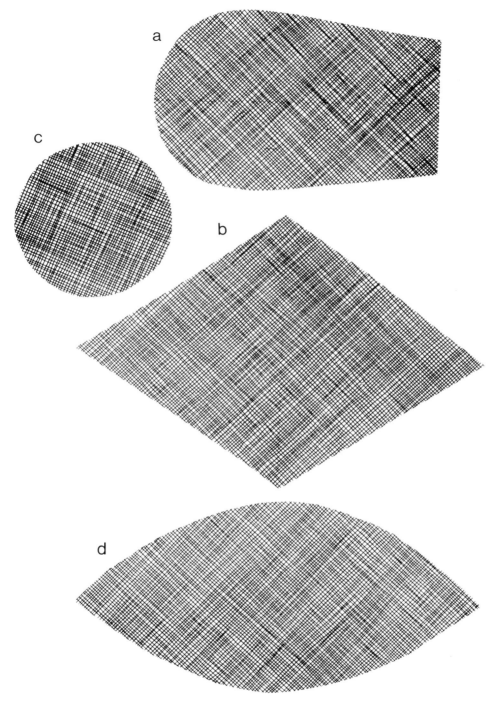

Fig. 2–9 Pattern for two floral appliques. Add ¼″ seam allowance to all pieces.

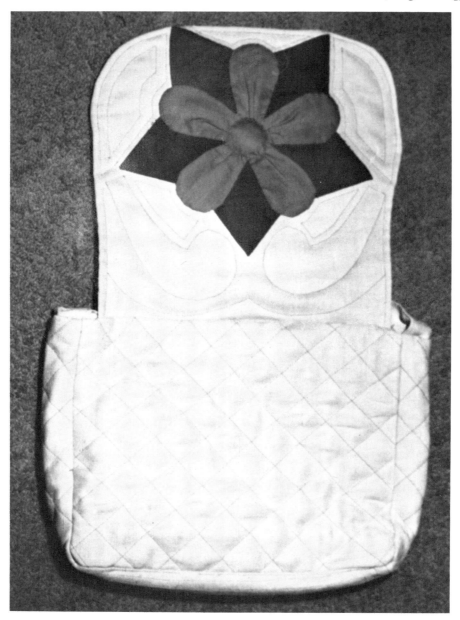

Fig. 2–10   Flap finished with appliqued flower and leaflets. Additional stitches in dark pink thread for quilting. Free-form design on flap, diamond pattern on back, sides, and front.

interlining and batting. Pull lining slightly to the underside. Press and baste around all edges, closing the raw edges of the top with basting stitches.

Step 4. See Figs. 1–4, 1–5, 1–9, and 2–10 for suggested decorative quilt stitching for the flap. The quilting techniques as described earlier will be stitched through the four layers of the flap. If hand stitching is to be employed, then use a thread color that is compatible with the outer fabric and lining. If machine stitching is to be used, then the outer fabric may have a thread color that is compatible with it and a bobbin thread of another color that can match the lining. All bags, whether quilted or made of very heavy fabrics, must have a row of stitches around the perimeter of the flap, approximately $1/3''$ to $1/2''$ off the folded edge. It is not necessary to stitch across the opening at the top. Set completed flap aside.

Step 5. To prepare the back, front, sides, and bottom piece, place each interlining piece on your work surface. Then lay the batting on top and trim all batting $1/2''$ smaller than the interlining. Place the outside fabric on top of each piece (matching the raw edges of the interlining and outer fabric) with right side to the ceiling. Baste around the edges $1/4''$ from the raw edge.

Step 6. For simple quilting, stitch as suggested in Fig. 2–11a. The heaviest quilting should be on the bottom, since this is the point of most stress.

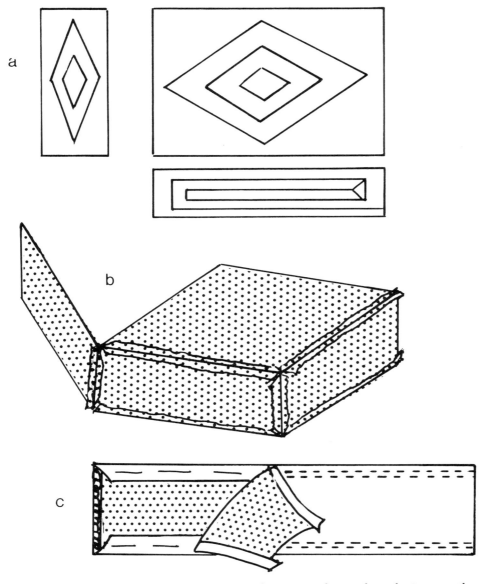

Fig. 2–11 Assembling the classic tote a. Suggested concentric line quilting. b. Sewing sides and bottom to back and front. c. Making the strap.

Step 7. Attach the bottoms of the two side pieces to the bottom piece with $1/2''$ seams. Place the two sides and bottom correspondingly against the front and stitch with a $1/2''$ seam all the way around, pivoting at the corners (Fig. 2–11*b*). Repeat to attach the back. Press seams open and trim excess from corners. Turn right-side-out and set aside.

Step 8. Turn the two long edges of the strap under $1/4''$ toward the wrong side and press. Trim both batting and interfacing to $3''$ wide and center them against the wrong side of the outer strap, lifting the folded seam allowance over them. Baste the two edges to hold the three layers in place (Fig. 2–11*c*). Turn in $1/4''$ on the two long edges of the strap lining and place it against the underside of the layered upper strap, wrong sides together. Baste to hold the edges even, then stitch by machine $1/4''$ off the edge. For extra strength, place another row of stitches $1/4''$ inside the first row (see both sides of Fig. 2–11*c*).

Step 9. To finish assembling the outer shell, baste the ends of the strap to the sides of the finished shell of the outer bag, making sure the right side of the strap is against the right side of the bag.

Step 10. With right sides together, place the raw edge of the flap against the raw edge of the top of the back of the outer shell. Baste through all layers $1/3''$ from the raw edge (Fig. 2–12). Trim any excess fabric out of the seam. Set shell aside.

Step 11. Attach pockets, if desired, to back piece of the lining. To make the entire lining, attach the bottoms of the two side pieces to the bottom piece with $1/2''$ seams. Place the two sides and bottom correspondingly against the "front" and stitch around the three sides with $1/2''$ seams, pivoting at the corners. Prepare the back for stitching the same way, but *stitch only the side pieces and $2''$ on each end of the bottom after pivoting the corners.* Leave an opening in the lining. Press. Use Fig. 2–11 as a guide.

Step 12. Slip the right side of the lining against the right side of the outer shell so the raw edges of the top will match and sew $1/2''$ around the top. Catch all the raw edges in the seam. Reinforce with extra stitching at the strap area (Fig. 2–13). Pull the entire bag right-side-out through the opening in the lining (see Fig. 2–14).

Step 13. Close the lining opening at the bottom with a few stitches and place the lining inside the bag. Starting at the side strap, place a row of machine stitches around the top, $1/4''$ down from the folded edge, to keep the lining from popping up. Ringing the top of the bag with stitches will also add durability to this point of stress.

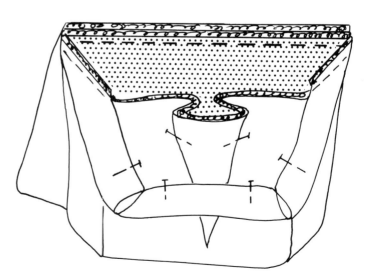

Fig. 2–12 Placing the strap against the sides and the flap against the back, right sides together. Baste.

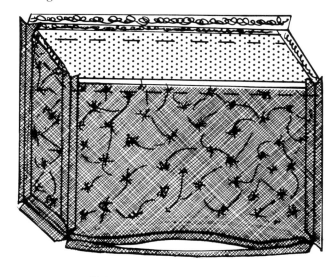

Fig. 2–13 Pull the outer shell of the bag through the opening in the lining.

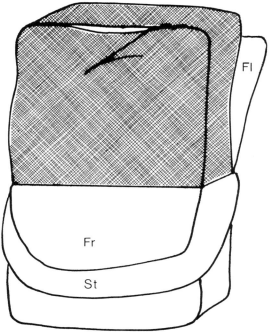

Fig. 2–14 Lining after being pulled through, before closing opening and being stuffed into bag.

Step 14. This bag would look good with a floorboard. See instructions earlier in this chapter for making floorboards.

BISCUIT BAG

This bag has its origin in the early American history of blanket making. Thirty-four little "biscuits" are made of fabric and stuffed separately. They are sewn together to form a bag that looks like a gay little patchwork quilt of squares (Figs. 2–15, 2–16, and color Fig. 10). This style is not limited to the 10″ x 14″ size or design shown here, but allows the maker to use a new set of designs each time it is made. This bag can be made totally

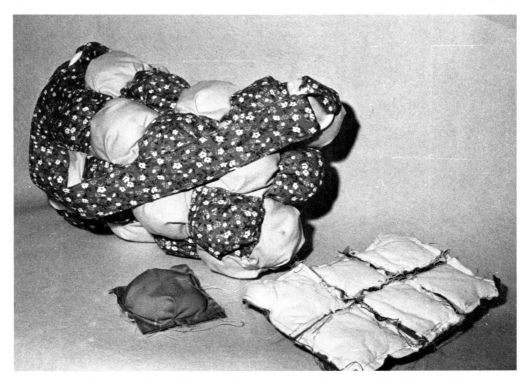

Fig. 2–15   Side view of biscuit bag; *at right*, one individual biscuit right-side-up and six biscuits joined together wrong-side-up.

of scrap fabrics. Bright and light colors in contrast are best to highlight the pattern of the little biscuits. Different prints combine well with each other in this old-fashioned bit of Americana.

MATERIALS

> outside fabric: 1 yard of 45″ of one color or ¹/₂ yard each of two colors, or ¹/₃ yard
>   each of three colors
> backing for biscuits: as above, or any scraps of sturdy fabric, drill, or ticking
> lining: ⁷/₈ yard of 45″ (strap is included in this measurement) or ⁵/₈ yard of 45″
>   without the strap. Lining will show, so it is best to pick a print to match the out-
>   side of bag
> washable belt interfacing: 2″ wide x 32″ long
> bag of *loose* polyester fiberfil or any washable pillow stuffing
> one snapper or Velcro dot closure, optional
> two rings, 2″ wide. With cotton type prints, colored plastics are suggested; with more
>   formal looking fabrics, metallic rings are smart

PREPARATION

Cut out two cardboard squares to use for patterns—one 4″ x 4″ and a second one 5″ x 5″. This includes the ¹/₄″ seam allowance. To use the patterns, draw the outlines on the right side of the fabrics. Cut out thirty-four squares from the outside fabric, using the larger pattern (two colors, as shown, will have seventeen solid and seventeen print), and thirty-four squares from the backing fabric, using the smaller pattern.

ASSEMBLY

Step 1. To form each little biscuit, place one large square on top of the smaller one, matching and pinning the corners, *wrong sides together.* Form tucks at the center of each large square on all four sides (Fig. 2–17a and b). Stitch ¼″ seams, beginning at * and ending at **. This leaves a small opening. From the bag of stuffing, take a good-sized fist-ful of filling material and place in the opening of the square. Sew the open corner closed. Repeat this process until you have thirty-four biscuits made.

Step 2. Stitch twelve squares together to form the front and twelve together to form the back (see Fig. 2–15). Place one biscuit face to face with the one you are attaching it to; keep the new stitch line one thread width to the inside of the first row of stitches that formed the biscuit puff. Work to assemble rows, then attach each row to the next. After

Fig. 2–16   Looking down into the bag. Note rickrack on inside pocket.

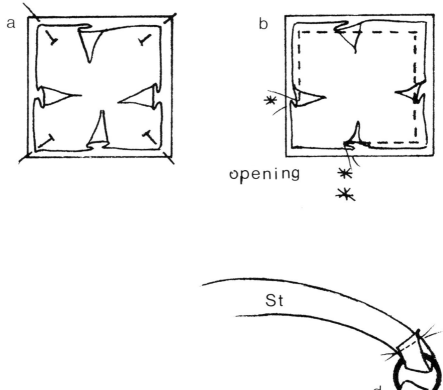

opening

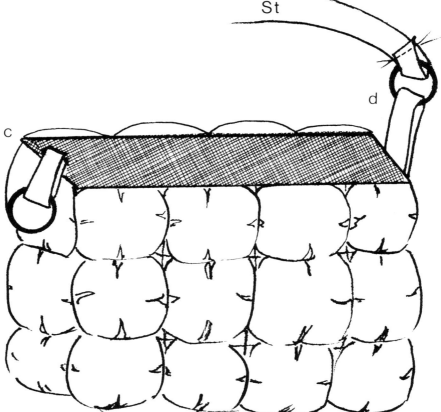

St

Fig. 2–17   a. Place the large piece of fabric on top of the smaller one, matching raw edges, and tucking upper fabric in the center at each side. b. Stitch ¼″ off edge, three-quarters of the way around, leaving one-quarter open. Stuff and sew closed. c. Putting tab on bag. d. Putting handle on ring.

making the front and back, assemble a row of ten biscuits. Place this row around the sides and bottom of the front first, then the back, working the seams on the wrong side.

Step 3. Cut two lengths of washable belt interfacing, 4″ long x 2″ wide, and two pieces of fabric used in the outer shell of the bag or of the lining, 5″ x 4″ long, to make two ring tabs. Wrap the 5″ width of outer fabric around the 2″ width of belt interfacing as described in strap method two (see Fig. 2–1b). Leave the 2″ ends raw. Fold each tab over each ring, bring the two raw ends of each tab together, and place the raw ends of the newly made ring tabs at each side of the bag and baste into place, allowing the ring to fall loose on the outside of the bag (Fig. 2–17c).

Step 4. Cut the lining of the bag, front and back, 11″ x 14″, and one long strip, 35½″ x 4″, ¼″ seam allowance included. Form into a square lining by stitching the long band around both 11″ sides and one 14″ bottom of front section. Repeat, attaching back the same way, but leave 9″ portion of the back bottom seam open (see Fig. 2–14). Slip the lining of the bag over the outside shell, with right sides together, and stitch all the way around the top, double stitching over the ring tabs at sides. Pull the outer shell through the opening in the lining and slipstitch the opening closed. Stuff the lining into the bag. With hidden hand stitching, catch the top perimeter of the lining against the back of the biscuits to hold it into the bag.

Step 5. Cut one strap of the same material as the tabs cut in step 4, 5″ x 25″. Cut one length of washable interlining, 2″ x 24″. Make a strap, using method two given earlier in this chapter (see Fig. 2–1b). Tuck the raw ends of each strap in against the wrong side of strap lining fabric so no raw edges show. Loop ends through the rings on either side of the bag. Secure the ends to the back of the strap on either side, by hand or machine stitching (Fig. 2–17d). A floorboard is suggested for the bottom of the bag. If you are desirous of closing the bag, use a Velcro or metal snap fastener. Attach it securely to the lining and the interlining of the biscuit behind it, at the center.

Because it is stuffed with polyester, just wash the entire bag in the gentle cycle of your washing machine. Dry in dryer on cool cycle.

VARIATIONS

For a young girl, it would be better to use only nine biscuits for front and back and nine around the sides and bottom. The biscuits could be of various sizes, from 1″ bottom and 1½″ top, right up to size given. The sides and bottom need not be biscuits, but could be made of heavily stiffened or quilted material, with the handle made of the same material.

RIGID-HANDLED KNITTING BAG

Fashion focuses once again on a roomy, sturdy old favorite—the knitting bag. This bag looks good in both glamour fabrics and country patchwork. The handles can be found in trimming stores and fabric shops everywhere. They can also be made from ¼″ or ⅜″ wood (pattern is given in Fig. 2–20) and stained or painted with glossy colors. Launch yourself on a nonstop fashion parade of handy, good looks. Make one to complement or match every costume (Figs. 2–18, 2–19 and color section).

MATERIALS (FOR SMALL SIZE)

    one set of rigid wood handles, 12″ to 14″ long
    ⅜ yard of 45″ outer fabric
    ⅔ yard of 30′ duck interlining
    ⅜ yard of lining
    13″ x 21″ of batting (optional)

Fig. 2–18   Rigid-handled knitting bags. Base fabric is cotton broadcloth with calico trims. This style has squared bottom and piping. *Made by Sonia Adams.*

Fig. 2–19   Rigid-handled knitting bags in classic gathered style. (*Top*) bag made of cotton and polyester sportswear broadcloth. (*Bottom, from left*) printed corduroy, *made by Annelie Klienen;* outlined quilted drapery print, *made by Mary Breitenbach.*

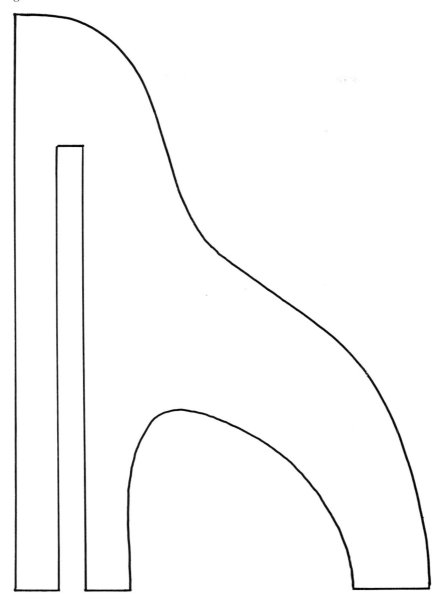

Fig. 2–20   One-half the pattern for rigid handle; cut from ¹/₄″ or ⁵/₈″ wood.

PREPARATION

Divide the outer fabric in half at the crosswise centerfold. It will equal two pieces 13¹/₂″ x 22″ for left and right outside; cut two interlining pieces, 12″ x 22″; cut two lining pieces 13″ x 22″.

ASSEMBLY

Step 1. Pin each piece of the interfacing against the wrong side of each outside fabric, matching on three sides. The interfacing will be short by 1¹/₂″ at top (Fig. 2–21*a*). If quilting is desired, it is at this point that the batting (¹/₂″ smaller on all sides than the interfac-

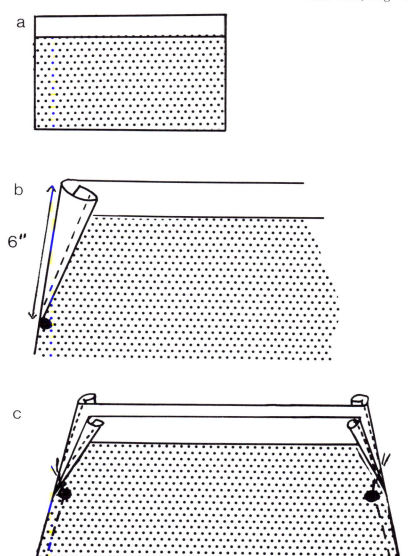

Fig. 2–21   a. Place the interfacing to the wrong side of the outer fabric, lining
up sides and bottom. b. Fold the top of the side opening over twice in a cone
shape, stopping at dot. c. Stitch around the outer edge of the bag, riding across
the dots and forming $^1/_4''$ to $^1/_2''$ seam.

ing) is slipped between the outer fabric and the interlining and the quilting is accomplished. Baste interlining to outside fabric on all four sides.

Step 2. Measure down from the top 6″ on both sides of a piece and mark with a pencil dot on interlining. Working from the top, turn in the raw edge $^1/_4''$ twice toward the
wrong side, graduating to nothing at the pencil dot (Fig. 2–21*b*). (If the outer fabric is
very thick, trim the interfacing out from under the first $^1/_4''$ fold.) Stitch down by machine
or hand. Repeat for the other side.

Step 3. Press down the raw edge of outside of bag at the top, $^1/_4''$ toward the wrong

Fig. 2–22 Making a squared-off corner. Top has stitching, bottom has been trimmed below stitching.

side and stitch ¹/₈″ off the raw edge. Turn and *press only* another 1¹/₂″ toward the wrong side. Repeat for the other side.

Step 4. Place the right sides of the front and back sections together. Match the dots on the sides. Begin the stitching so that it runs across the dot on the righthand side and continues down the side, around the bottom, and up the other side with a ¹/₂″ seam. When approaching the second dot, slant the stitches to again run off the seam allowance crossing the dot (Fig. 2–21c).

Step 5. To square off the bottom, have the shell of the bag inside out. Pick up a corner and fold side seam against the bottom seam to form a point (Fig. 2–22). Measure down 1¹/₂″ from the point and stitch straight across and back again for extra strength. Trim excess point beyond stitching, leaving a ¹/₄″ seam. Repeat for the other corner. Turn right-side-out and the outer bag has squared-off corners.

Step 6. Add an inside pocket of your choice to the lining, as discussed earlier in this chapter. The pocket should be of the open type and should be placed in the center and very low, with its bottom about 3″ from the raw edge of the bottom seam allowance.

Step 7. On the wrong side of the lining fabric, measure down from the top 5″ and place a pencil dot at each side seam. Turn in ¹/₄″ two times on each side from top to the dot, toward the wrong side. Allow the fold to graduate to nothing past the dot. Stitch from the top, running off the fabric as in Fig. 2–21b and c of outer bag. Repeat for the other side. The lining is made very similar to outer side. Skip step 3, then continue to prepare the lining following steps 4 and 5 of the outer bag and press when finished.

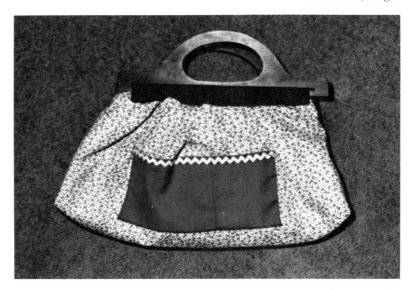

Fig. 2–23 Securing outer shell of the bag to the handles; bring outside through slot in handle and hand stitch to lining and interlining, or machine stitch across.

Step 8. Place the lining inside the outer bag, with wrong sides together. Note that the lining will not come to the top of the outer shell of the bag. Match the side opening and stitch together by hand with a blind stitch. Baste the lining into place across front and back near top of lining.

Step 9. Place the top of each outer side in the lower opening in the handles. Pull the outer side to the inside, using the 1¼″ fold made in step 3 as a guide. Arrange the gathers evenly. The top of the outer edge of the shell will overlap the lining. Stitch by hand, securing the top edge to the interlining permanently and pulling gathers to one side, then the other, as you stitch (Fig. 2–23). Do not allow the stitches to come through to the outer fabric of the bag. Gathers should look like they fall loosely from the opening in the handle. Or machine stitch with big stitches through all layers on each side. When bag needs to be laundered, remove from handles.

VARIATION

This bag looks smart with the sides and bottom piped and not squared off as in step 5. See Fig. 2–18 of calico applique and piping. Before proceeding with step 4, place piping against front of bag, running ends of piping off to the dots on the sides. Then proceed with step 4. Skip step 5 and proceed with step 6. This bag is also smart as a large tote. See color Fig. 4, beige bag with horse applique.

DOWEL-HANDLED BAG

This large capacity, soft crushed pouch takes well to the widest variety of fabrics. Its rigid double handles are made of wood in a variety of constructions (Figs. 2–24 and 2–25). First, two old-fashioned wooden dowels are capped on the ends with large decorative knobs, mini finials (used for cafe curtain rods), blocks of wood, small decorative drawer pulls, or wooden beads. By capping the ends of the dowels you are, in effect, holding the bag on the dowels. (See color Fig. 4.)

Fig. 2–24   Dowel-handled bag in a printed drapery fabric.

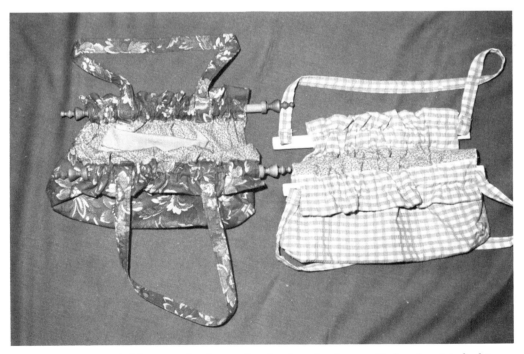

Fig. 2–25   Bag at left has mini-finial capped ends, the other has a split dowel, painted white.

Large wooden beads will have to be fitted over the ends of the dowels and glued with good wood glue. The finials and drawer pulls have screws fitted into the ends and can be screwed onto the dowels. This is an optional feature, depending on what can be found in your area. Try hardware stores, drapery supply departments, craft shops, or even furniture and cabinet accessories departments.

The second method is less dressy but extremely serviceable. Using a 1″ to 1½″ dowel or window shade roller, split it in half lengthwise. Cut it 15″ to 17″ long for the pattern measurements given. Drill a ½″ diameter hole, ½″ from each end of the split dowels. These holes will be used to secure the strap ends through and, in effect, hold the bag on the split dowels. If you do not have a large ½″ drill bit for making holes, use two smaller ones side by side and file into an oval opening.

This bag can be made in a variety of sizes. The pattern given is for a large-capacity daytime use, but the basic rectangle can be made shallow for late-day and evening bags or deeper for beach bags.

MATERIALS

outside fabric: 1 yard of 45″. This does not allow for a one-way print, such as people figures who have to stand up. This is a good bag for corduroy, velour, velvet, as well as cotton types
lining: 1 yard, 45″ width
interlining: 1 yard, 30″ width
two dowels, ½″ x 15″ to 17″ long, or a shade roller 1″ wide x 15″ to 17″ long
washable belt interlining, ½″ wide x 65″ long
four knobs, to be used as discussed above, *optional*

PREPARATION

After the handles are selected, they may be stained and a coat of varnish added for gloss, or they may be painted, preferably with a high-gloss enamel. For a small supply of high-fashion color, use the model paints found in hobby or toy departments.

Step 1. Cut one piece of outside fabric 22″ wide by 32″ long (seam allowance included). Cut interlining exactly 21″ x 32″, center and baste loosely to the wrong side of the outer fabric. Turn the two 22″ edges ½″ to the wrong side, over the interlining, press, and stitch close to the edge. (Use Fig. 2–26 as a guide.) Consider these two edges the top edges of the bag. Measure down 10″ from the top. Place a pencil dot on the interlining on all four top edges (see Fig. 2–21b). Working from the top, turn in the raw edge of the sides ¼″ twice toward the wrong side, diminishing the fold to nothing at the pencil dot (similar to Fig. 2–21b). If the outer fabric is very thick, trim the interfacing out

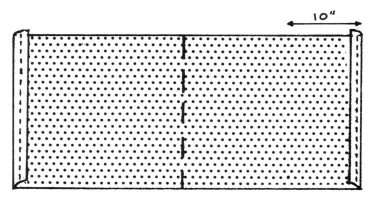

Fig. 2–26 Place the interlining into wrong side of outer fabric, turn top edges, mark center with basting, and measure down 10″ from all four top edges.

from under the fold. Stitch down by machine or hand. Repeat for the other three sides.

Step 2. Fold the bag in half with right sides together. Mark the center bottom fold line with a row of basting stitches through both fabrics. Stitch the sides, working from the bottom, making ¹/₂" seams that diminish to nothing, crossing the dots on the side of the bag, similar to Fig. 2–21c.

Step 3. To square off the bottom, have the shell of the bag inside out. Pick up one corner and fold the side seam against the basting stitches at the bottom of the bag, forming a point (see Fig. 2–22). Measure down 1¹/₂" from the point and stitch straight across and back again for extra strength. Trim the excess point beyond stitching, leaving a ¹/₄" seam. Repeat for the other corner. Turn right-side-out and the outer shell of the bag has a squared-off bottom.

Step 4. Cut the lining 18" x 22". With right sides together, fold this rectangle in half so you have a rectangle 22" x 9". Press, unfold, and mark this fold with a large basting stitch. Center any pocket of your choice on one half of the right side of the lining fabric (suggest 4" x 8" pocket). With the right sides together, fold in half again and stitch side seams closed with ¹/₂" seams, stopping 2" from the top raw edges at each side. Square off the corners of the lining as you did for the outer shell of the bag in step 3. Place the lining inside the outer shell of the bag with wrong sides together. The lining will be shorter. Turn the raw edges of side openings to wrong side. Press. Match the V-shaped opening at the side and stitch lining to outer shell by hand or machine along both side openings. Baste the raw edges of the lining to the outer shell to hold it in its proper place along front and back. Set aside.

Step 5. Cut two straps, 2" wide by 26" long. Lay pieces of ¹/₂"-wide washable belt interfacing in the center and use strap method two detailed earlier (see Fig. 2–1b). If you are using the split dowel handle and straps are to be placed in holes at the end of the dowels, then turn the narrow end of each strap to wrong side while it is being made. If you are using double dowels with capped ends, then the ends of the straps may be left raw.

Step 6. *Strap attachment for solid dowels with capped ends* (go to step 7 for split dowel attachment). Fold the top edge of the outer shell of the bag 3" toward the inside. The lower edge should be covering the raw edges of the lining. Pin in place (Fig. 2–27, point *). Along this folded edge, measure 5" from both side openings. Place two pins. Insert the two raw ends of the strap in a U-shaped position and stitch across permanently, placing the stitches ¹/₈" inside the folded edges and stitching through all layers. Fold the strap upward and secure with pins. Measure down 1¹/₄" inches from the top fold and place another line of *basting* stitches across (Fig. 2–27, point **), crossing them over to hold the straps in an upright position. Slip the whole dowel, or split dowel into the casing just made between points * and ** to make sure that the dowel fits. The permanent stitches can be adjusted to either side of the basting to accommodate the dowel. Remove dowel and stitch permanently. Repeat for other side. Place a dowel cut 15" to 17" long into the casing and apply the selected four ends to dowels.

The trick is to make the fabric gather comfortably over the wood, without looking bunched or too tight. As fabric and dowel size will vary, so will the casing measurement between * and ** in Fig. 2–27.

Step 7. *Strap attachment for split dowels.* Disregard the strap inset if you are using the split dowel technique. Just place the two rows of stitches across, forming a casing for dowel as directed in step 6. After all adjustments have been made, then repeat for the other side (see Fig. 2–27). Slip the two dowel halves into the casing, placing the rounded edge to the outside and the flat sides together to the inside of the bag. Gather the bag to the center and slip the straps through the end holes from the outside to the inside (Fig.

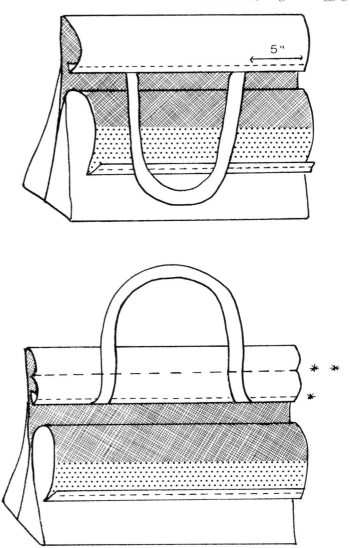

Fig. 2–27 Strap attach-
ment for dowels with
capped ends. (*Top*) set-
ting in the strap; (*bottom*)
forming the casing for
the dowel.

2–28). Loop each end of the strap so that it catches on the back of the strap, then machine stitch or secure by hand. Repeat for the second dowel.

VARIATIONS

This bag can be made any size and would be excellent as a big beach bag, cutting the initial rectangle of fabric 26″ x 50″, or it would make an excellent small puffy bag by cutting the fabric 14″ x 20″ and placing it on small 8″ dowels capped at the ends with beads or jeweled buttons.

SHAPED SPLIT-STRAP SHOULDER BAG

The ultimate in versatility is this all-occasion styling (Fig. 2–29). (See color Fig. 9, bag styled in brown with harness latch, beige with rickrack trim, and orange linen with crewel embroidery.) The bag sports a strap that can be made with belt fastenings—mock

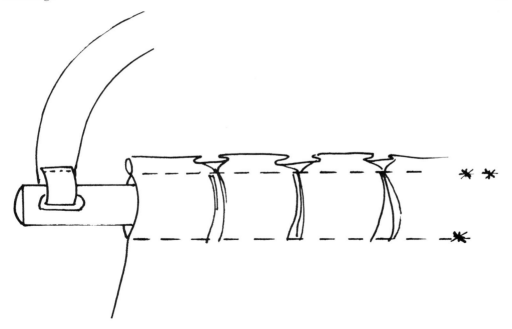

Fig. 2–28 Place strap in split dowel and loop to catch on back, then secure.

Fig. 2–29 Split-strap shoulder bag, trimmed in rickrack with outside pocket and zipper top.

or real—which allow for the adjustment of the strap. If security is important, then a wide zipper can be added to close the top. This is not a beginner bag.

If roomy compartments are needed, this styling can be made with additional outside front pockets for books, newspapers, or glasses. Styled without the pocket, the front can be a place to show off your needlepoint, embroidery, crewel, or applique skills. This bag is good looking when quilted with a contrsting color thread throughout, or it can have the sides quilted only. Study the photos of this bag and decide on the optional features that will best suit your needs. Optional features are step 3, the front pocket; step 6, the insertion of a zipper; and step 7, the harness latch. Even in step 9 there are optional features to consider. Versatility is unlimited, with many unshown suggestions offered. It is up to the craft designer to apply creativity. Approximate size is 5″ at bottom and 10″ high x 16″ wide.

MATERIALS

  outside: ³/₄ yard of 45″ (not allowing for one-way design)
  lining: ³/₄ yard of 45″
  interlining: 1 yard
  batting for a quilted look, 27″ x 45″ (optional)
  washable belt interlining, 60″ x 2″
  optional: mock or real buckle closure, 2″ opening inside; zipper, 12″ separating, with
      wide side tapes; harness latch and matching ring (2″ size suggested)

PREPARATION

If any trim is planned, prepare the outside fabric first. If you wish to embroider or applique the front of the bag, then it would be wise to cut a piece for the front of the bag (10″ x 16″), larger than called for by the pattern, making sure that you can get it into your embroidery frame securely. Do the embroidery, then cut out exactly to fit the bag.

If you plan to use rickrack or ribbon trims, draw the lines for them on the front and back very carefully. The large additional pocket is made of two pieces, so trim can be placed on only the piece that will show. If rickrack is used, pin on front first, secure each point and each indentation by hand, using a double length of thread, working from the wrong side. If giant rickrack is used, outline each edge with a small stitch on the machine.

The outer fabric may be trimmed with fancy novelty stitches made by the newer machines. Experiment. If you like a particular stitch but feel it is a little weak-looking by itself, then make three or four rows of the same stitch in the same color, then move on to the next stitch in a different color; perhaps only two rows of another stitch will be needed. The variations are unlimited. If you are inclined to delightful handwork, soutache braid or homemade frogging can be used in a planned or random design and applied by hand.

ASSEMBLY

Step 1. Pattern for open shoulder bag with pocket front. *Pattern is given with no seam allowance, but ¹/₂″ seam allowance is suggested.* (Use Fig. 2–30 as a guide for measurements.) Cut one front and back A, each 10″ high x 14″ at top x 16″ at bottom, of outside fabric, lining, and interlining. *Note:* The broken line across front piece A is for an optional front pocket. Make a separate pattern piece AA for the front pocket, 7″ high x 14¹/₂″ at top x 16″ at bottom. Cut two pockets from the outside fabric and one interlining. The bottom piece is B, 16″ long by 5″ wide. Cut one bottom from outside fabric, one lining, and one interlining. The long side and strap are combined into single pattern piece C, 36″ long, 5″ wide at bottom sloping to 2″ wide, 10″ above bottom. From the base, measure up 10″, put a double line as shown to mark the side bag portion. The other 26″ is

Fig. 1   Soft knit beret on a band made of wool double knit; toque of white fake fur; mini-madcap marvel of polyester double knit, trimmed with felt flower.

Fig. 2   Envelope bags. (*Left to right, from top*) evening bag of gold brocade; black velvet with gold trim; square of brown upholstery fabric; white linen envelope with appliqued flower; bag of red needlepoint upholstery.

Fig. 3   Nomad luggage: all styles in water-repellent canvas. Dress bag of turquoise and single suiter in yellow, both trimmed with double-fold braid in contrasting colors; triple-pocket jiffy shopper, trimmed with braid and cotton daisy-embroidered ribbon; solid-color flight bag.

Fig. 4 (*Clockwise from top*) small version of ring-handled pouch made in black wool with bamboo rings; double-pocket mini bag made of canvas; double dowel-handled bag of printed cotton drapery fabric; dowel-handled bag in cotton and polyester seersucker on split dowel. On the floor is a rigid-handled knitting bag, extra large version with wood handles, made of heavy beige drapery linen with polished cotton applique; above it is the standard size in solid green trigger cloth. Peeking out from behind is the paisley print hobo.

Fig. 5 Nomad travel styles. Canvas carryall in red with embroidered ribbon trim, seams also finished with double-fold braid; duffle of off-white drill cloth, trimmed with royal blue piping and multicolored luggage webbing straps; backpack of quilted patchwork print, seams trimmed with double-fold braid.

Fig. 6 Classic flapped tote of linen, trimmed with a floral applique.

Fig. 7 (*From left*) wool plaid English auto cap; trainman's caps in solid blue-jean denim and striped denim; men's version of the international unisex hat.

Fig. 8 Tie-back style in white satin; pull-on turban of matte jersey with a brooch; black velvet French beret, trimmed with striped bow.

Fig. 9 Three versions of the split-strap shoulder bag. On chair are brown chevron-weave upholstery fabric with harness latch closure and orange linen bag with crewel embroidery, trimmed with white leather-covered mock buckle. The same bag is repeated at left on floor in beige sportswear cotton and polyester broadcloth, made with an outside pocket and zip-top closure and trimmed with rickrack. At right, the fake fur bag with a double gold chain.

Fig. 10   Matching hats 'n bags. Striped calico patchwork reversible bag and matching English auto hat; open-crown peaked hat and biscuit bag in green and yellow print; open-crown brimmer with matching convertible beachmat and bag in printed chintz; sundowner with matching classic tote bag in off-white muslin trimmed with petal applique.

Fig. 11   Two-pocket accordion bag of dress-weight wool and polyester broadcloth, quilted in a diamond pattern.

Fig. 12   Variation on the rope ringer with rigid handle. This version is of patchwork print with large quilting through the squares.

Fig. 13   Cloche in pink washable velvet, trimmed with a flower; snail in gray wool jersey; snood (pattern not supplied)

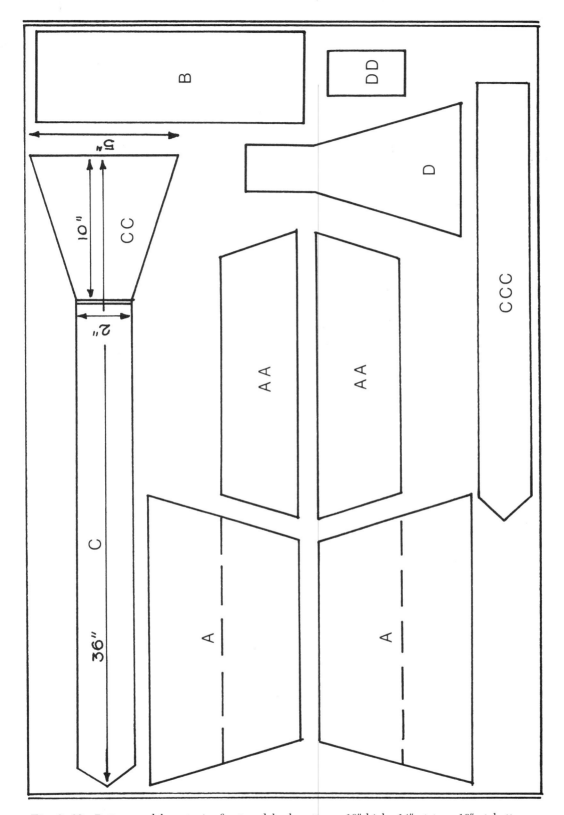

Fig. 2–30 Pattern and layout. A—front and back pattern, 10″ high, 14″ at top, 16″ at bottom. AA—optional two-piece pocket, 7″ high, 14½″ at top, 16″ at bottom. B—bottom, 5″ x 16″. C—long side and strap, 36″ long overall, 5″ wide at bottom; measure up 10″ on center line to form 2″ neck. CC—the inside lining of the bag. Use the lower portion, 5″ wide at bottom, 10″ high, and 2″ wide at top. CCC—lining to strap, cut from outside fabric, 26″ long x 2″ wide. D—short side and strap. Cut exactly as C, but only 16″ long, measuring up from the bottom. DD—lining of outside fabric for D, 6½″ x 2″.

the strap portion. Cut one piece of the outer fabric and interlining *complete* from C, 36″ long. Then, using only the lower 10″ (below the double line) as the pattern, cut two lining pieces CC. The long strap will have to have a lining. In all the samples photographed, the outside fabric was used as a lining. Cut one piece 26″ long by 2″ wide to line the strap. Call this CCC.

The short side and strap are given as pattern piece D. Use pattern piece C as a model for D. Make pattern 16″ long. Cut one piece from the outside fabric and one interlining. To line this strap, cut a piece of outside fabric 6½″ long x 2″ wide. Call this DD. For all pattern dimensions and suggested pattern layout, see Fig. 2–30.

Step 2. Against the wrong side of each of the outer pieces, place the matching interlining. If quilting is to be the fashion approach to your bag, then slip the batting in between the outside and the interlining; add quilt lines, using a diamond pattern or outlining the print. This adds support. Center a band of washable belt interfacing on pieces C and D, allowing the belt interfacing to run the length of each piece and into the seam allowance at the wide bottom ends of both.

Step 3. Optional front pocket: Place single interfacing AA against the wrong side of one of the two outer pockets AA. Baste together and treat as one piece. Place the right sides of the two pockets AA together and stitch across the narrow end (Fig. 2–31). Turn

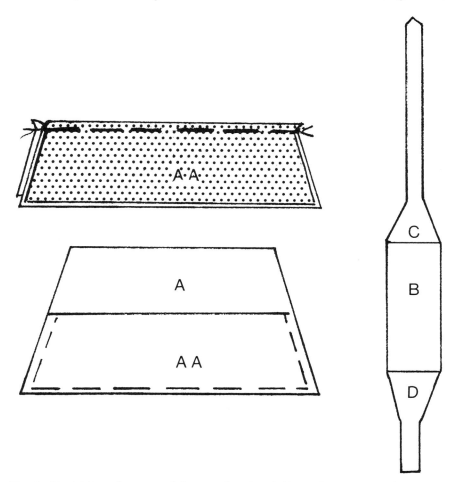

Fig. 2–31   Making the optional front pocket: (*top left*) sew lining to outside at top; (*bottom left*) baste to outside; (*right*) attaching perimeter pieces.

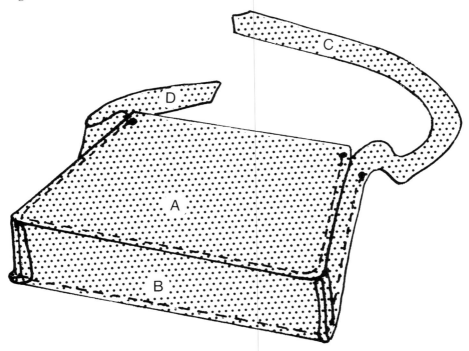

Fig. 2–32   Placing sides and bottom against front (view from wrong-side-out). Note dots near top to indicate where to start and stop stitching side seams at cross point of both seams.

to the right side. If quilting is to be accomplished, slip the batting between the interlining and the wrong side of the piece to be the outside. Baste all remaining raw edges together and quilt through the four layers. If quilting is not planned, just baste together, run one row of stitches across the top, $1/2''$ from the edge. This will form the pocket. Place this newly formed pocket against outside front piece A and baste the side and bottom raw edges together. This will be the front of the bag (Fig. 2–31).

Step 4. Stitch the 5″ ends of C and D to either narrow end of pattern piece B, forming one long strip (Fig. 2–31).

Step 5. Match the remaining seam allowance of B to the bottom of the front of A. Bring the C and D sides up along the sides of the front of A, allowing the strap portion to hang loose. Baste and stitch, starting and stopping at the seam allowance at the top of either side (Fig. 2–32). Attach the back in the same manner. Press seams open lightly before turning right-side-out. Baste back the remaining raw seam allowance on the top of the two A pieces (front and back), *if no zipper is to be added.* Baste back the seam allowance on the two side straps, trimming out the interlining where necessary if it's too bulky.

The next two features are optional. The bag doesn't need a closure. It can be left open. If step 6, the zipper, is used, omit step 7, the harness latch closure, or vice-versa. If both are omitted, skip to step 8, the lining.

Step 6. Optional zipper. Purchase a 12″ separating zipper with wide side tapes, metal preferred. Separate the zipper and center one tape against the front and one against the back, the edge of tape against the raw edge of bag (Fig. 2–33). Tuck the raw ends of the tapes to wrong side and baste across each top. Stitch permanently *within the seam allowance.* Turn the seam allowance and the zipper tape to the inside of the bag, and baste tape edge against bag interlining. The zipper will be standing up—this is right.

Step 7. Optional harness latch (Fig. 2–34). To make the tabs, measure the width of

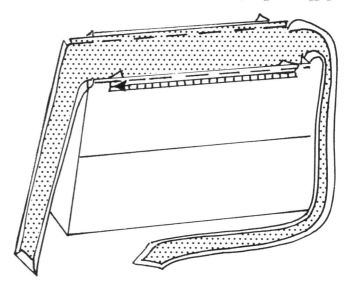

Fig. 2–33 Centering optional
zipper on front and back.

the ring opening at the top end of your latch. Double that and add your seam allowance.
This will be the width needed for the tab. Cut the tab about 18″ long, or longer if you
plan to carry a great deal of paraphernalia. With right sides together, fold in half lengthwise (18″) and stitch on the seam allowances. Press seam open. Turn right side out and
roll this tubing so the seam appears in the middle rather than on the side, and press (Fig.
2–35*a*). While at the ironing board, fold one raw end of the tubing to the wrong side and
press. Slip the newly made tab through the ring end of the latch and fold in half crosswise

Fig. 2–34   Split-strap shoulder bag with optional harness latch closure.

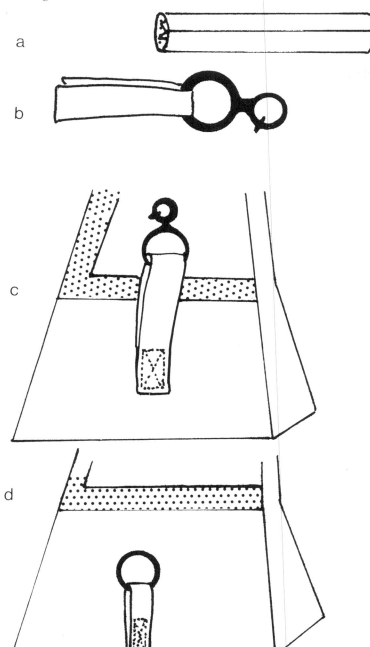

Fig. 2–35 Attaching
harness latch a. Make
fabric tubing with seam
in center to form tabs.
b. Fold tab through
loop in harness latch. c.
Attach tab to back of bag.
d. Fold remainder of tab
through the ring. Attach
to front of bag.

(Fig. 2–35*b*). Pin with a safety pin to hold in place. Place the folded tab against the back of the bag close to the top, so that latch falls over the front. Center the two tab ends against the back, the finished end on top, and stitch approximately a 2″ square to secure tab to back (Fig. 2–35*c*).

Do the same with an 8″ length of fabric for the ring on the front of the bag. Leave both ends of the tab raw. Centering the ring tab on the front, open a few stitches in the bottom front seam, slip the raw ends into it, and restitch. Reinforce with a few stitches

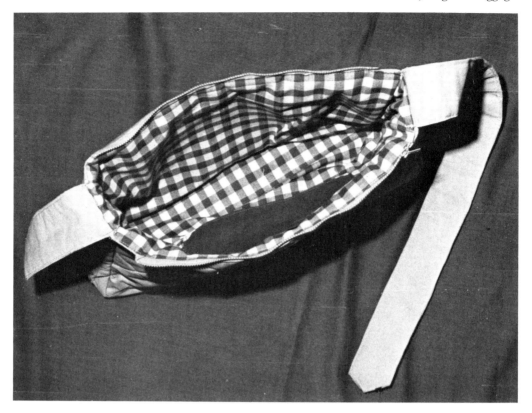

Fig. 2–36   Placing lining into the bag, viewed from above. Note that lining for straps matches outside fabric, lining for inside is checked, and pocket is solid color. Alternate option is to have lining made from same fabric as outside.

below ring (Fig. 2–35*d*). When the bag is open, the latch should be lifted to the back. The tabs and latch should fit smoothly over the top and front. That is why it is applied after the bag has been assembled. It is adjusted depending on size of latch purchased.

Step 8. Making the lining. Seam together the CCC strap lining to the side of lining CC and repeat for the DD lining to the second CC lining piece. This will then resemble the pieces of the outside shell. Attach to the bottom at narrow end. Proceed to assemble exactly as in step 5. Finish by basting the entire perimeter seam allowance to the wrong side. Slip the lining into the bag, wrong sides together, matching outside (Fig. 2–36). Baste across front, back, and strap in one continuous line, then topstitch, pivoting at the corners. Use matching colored thread in bobbin and top. It is best to use about 12 to 15 stitches to the inch. A second row of stitching can be added beyond the first for strength, especially in the strap area. A floorboard is suggested.

Step 9. Closing the strap. Adjust the strap to proper length, closing the long pointed end over the short blunt end. Use one of these treatments to finish.

1. Close with permanent stitches or novelty jewelry pin.

2. Slip a mock buckle onto the long strap end and stitch above and below buckle to hold in place permanently.

3. Make a machine buttonhole and use a regular buckle with a shank. Place shank through the buttonhole and fold back end around shank bar. Make small buttonhole in other side of the strap to accommodate shank itself.

ENVELOPE

Dashing, distinctive, and always in fashion, this slim, lightweight envelope takes very little yardage. It's shown here with three different construction methods. (See color Fig. 2 and Fig. 2–37.) First, the one-piece construction good for daytime and heavyweight fabrics; second, the one-piece construction reinforced with a firming inter-liner called Permette. This interliner is found in drapery supply departments and is used to make rather firm-looking cornices. This product, or any like it, enables the handbag crafter to supply to very soft fabrics the additional support that is needed for the sleek envelope styling. It is particularly good to use with evening bag fabrics. Finally, the three-part construction is excellent for working out special design effects from pieces of fabric with large patterns. This is shown in color Fig. 2, the red envelope with the floral design centered on the flap, back, and front. Originally, it was a large piece of upholstery with a widely spaced floral design. Each of the floral motifs were cut from the fabric separately. Needlepoint canvas, embroidery, applique, or special highlights of a drapery print or upholstery type fabric can be worked out effectively with this construction, plac-ing the design on the front flap only, or exactly where you want it.

Once you understand these simple constructions, you can translate the easy patterns into dozens of bags. There are no yardage requirements given because it is basically only one rectangle of fabric and can easily be figured to fit your needs. Special effects will have to be considered individually.

PLANNING A PATTERN

Since there are no side or bottom insets to be concerned with, begin planning the back, front, and flap. Most often these bags are found in a rectangular shape, but don't let that hold you back from designing a square one or one with a round bottom (see color

Fig. 2–37   Envelope styling. Black canvas trimmed with double-fold braid and luggage webbing.

Fig. 2, gold brocade). Most often, envelopes are carried in the hand, but they can sport straps for a novel look. The small evening styles are stunning dangling on metallic chain, to be found in belt and jewelry departments of local shops (see color Fig. 2, black velvet).

The design of the flap or the glamorous appeal of the fabric sets the tone for the bag. Use this equation: The plainer the fabric, the more interest must lie in the flap shape; the more eye appeal to the fabric, the simpler the flap shape.

To make a pattern for the simplest one-piece construction, measure one rectangle for the front. Suggested sizes are 6″ x 9″, 8″ x 11″, or 10″ x 10″. Join to it, in the exact size, a rectangle for the back, and join to it again the same measurement for the flap (Fig. 2–38*a*). Then pencil in the shape of the flap. Add seam allowances all the way around the perimeter. This pattern can be strengthened with an interfacing, such as drill or canvas, and that will be cut exactly as the outside fabric, including the seam allowances. To achieve a very firm construction, this one-piece pattern will use semirigid *interlining*, such a Permette. When cutting this interlining, do not add a seam allowance to the Permette as it is too difficult to stitch through. The *linings* for both of the above will be cut with the seam allowance the same as the outside fabric. See chart below.

To make a pattern for the three-piece construction suggested for highlighting needlework or upholstery, draw one rectangle, plus seam allowance all the way around, and use that for the cutting of both the back and the front and the flap, separately, or trace that piece out again and design a shaped flap (Fig. 2–38*b*). For the *interlining and lining*, cut the three pattern pieces as the outside. See Fig. 2–38*c*, showing a finished bag, using the three-part construction. Shown here are the flap at the top and back of bag, with braided strap.

When designing the flap, make sure that it is either the full length of the front and back measurement, or at least two-thirds the length of the front. If the flap is too short, it is hard to keep the bag closed and things will be spilling out.

CUTTING CHART

Pattern	Outside Fabric	Interlining, such as Drill	Permanent Firm Interlining	Lining
a—One-piece soft construction	1	1	—	1
b—One-piece firm construction	1	—	1	1
c—Three-piece construction	3	3	—	3

ASSEMBLY

Step 1. Baste the standard interlinings against the wrong side of the outside fabric. If using the Permette interlining, proceed to work without it. It can be put into the bag later. If working the three-piece construction, baste each interlining to its respective outside, then stitch the pieces together permanently, front to back, and back to flap. Press seams open and treat as one long piece.

Step 2. Fold the front against the back, right sides together. On the wrong side, stitch up to the *top seam allowance*, but not through it, on both sides (note large dots in Fig. 2–39). Repeat this step for the lining. Baste back the front seam allowance to the wrong side on both outer shell and lining. If the interlining seems bulky, trim it out of seam allowances and clip out excess bulk from bottom corners of bag in both seam allowances. Keep the bag in the wrong-side-out position.

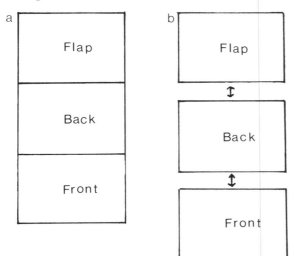

a

Flap

Back

Front

b

Flap

↕

Back

↕

Front

Fig. 2–38   Envelope layout a. All-in-one construction; seam allowance around outside only. b. Three-piece construction; seam allowance around each piece. c. Finished closeup of three-piece construction, shown with flap open at top. Note seam joining flap to back. Made of red upholstery fabric.

c

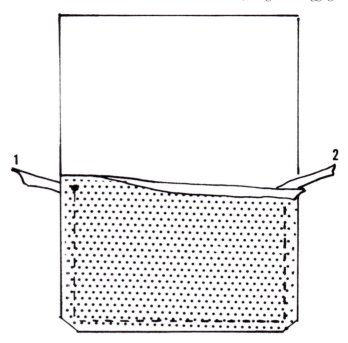

Fig. 2–39 Joining front to back. Turn upper front seam allowance to wrong side and place strap in pocket formed by front and back, with ends exposed at points 1 and 2.

Step 3. If the bag is to have a handle of chain, braid, self material, crochet, or macrame, place the main portion of the strap inside the lower shell of the bag, allowing the raw ends to stick out at points 1 and 2 (Fig. 2–39). Pin or baste in place securely.

Step 4. Use Fig. 2–40 as a guide: With right sides together, place the flap portion of the lining against the flap portion of the outside fabric; pin in place. The lower (back and front) portions of both lining and outer shell will be hanging free. Stitch around the lining, starting at point 1, catching the optional strap in the stitching. Stitch on the seam line around the flap, finishing at point 2. Fig. 2–40 shows the lining drawn back a bit. When the seaming has been completed, trim corners and pull the newly lined flap and lower shell both to the outside. At this point, the optional Permette can be slipped into the flap section between wrong sides of lining and outer fabric, and slipped down between back and front of the bag (Fig. 2–41).

The lower portion of lining can then be slipped into the lower shell of the bag and adjusted. Press. The two basted-back seam allowances of the front outer shell and front lining will meet. They can be pinned or basted together, then machine topstitched or blind stitched by hand.

Step 5. Finishing tricks: The best way to close this bag is to use a snap or Velcro dot. It is best to sew this to the flap front after the bag is finished and pressed. Catch the lining and interlining, but not the outside fabric. Tabs with heavy medallions can be used or small buckles applied. The flap of the bag can be topstitched $1/8''$ to $1/2''$ from the edge, whichever looks best.

REVERSIBLE BAG

The diplomat of all bags is one that can do a quick change. This tailored reversible daytime bag converts from a jaunty strip patchwork to a serviceable denim trimmed with a purchased embroidered applique (Figs. 2–42 and 2–43). The novelty shape will flatter

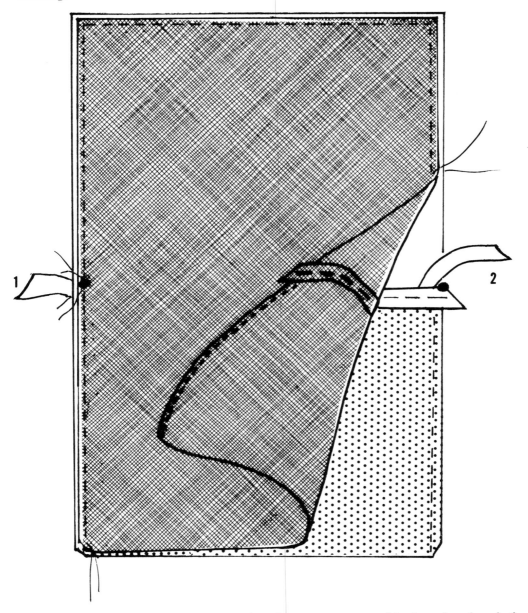

Fig. 2–40 Setting the lining into the envelope bag. Lining is turned back to show how both turned-back seam allowances of front are placed on top of each other. Note dots on flap portion. Sew from 1 to 2 over the sides and top of flap.

any fabric and easily takes on the short or long strap. Now is the time to invest in two very special outside fabrics to match a host of fashion apparel in your closet. (See color Fig. 10 for stripe-look bag, along with matching English auto hat.)

MATERIALS

$3/4$ yard each of two different fabrics for the outsides (sample used a patchwork design of scraps cut and assembled into strips for one side and denim for reverse side)

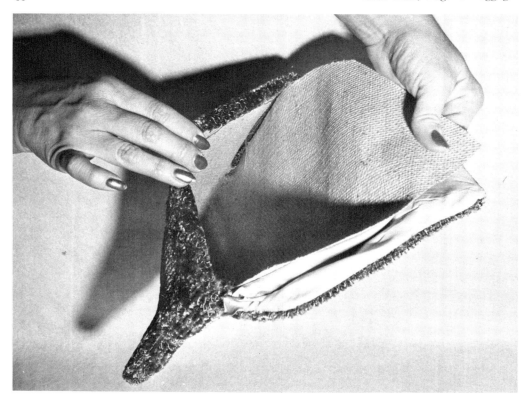

Fig. 2–41   Slip the optional Permette interlining into bottom of bag first, then slip lower lining over it and work remainder into flap.

3/4 yard of 30″ interfacing or 1/2 yard of 45″
20″ x 32″ piece of batting (optional, if quilting)
1 yard of 1″-wide washable belt interfacing

PREPARATION

To Make the Pattern. Use Fig. 2–44 as a guide: On 1″-grid graph paper, 20″ x 18″, draw a line down the center 20″ long. Working from *one side only*, measure down from the top 3″. Place a dot. Measure out 5″ to the right and place a dot. Join the dot at the top to dot just made with a slanted line. Working from the top of the 20″ line, measure down 9″ and place a dot. Measure out to the right 4″—place a dot and add to that line another inch; place a small square. Join the newly made dot to the dot above. This will form the flap portion of the bag. Draw a broken line horizontally from the center to small square.

Working from the bottom of the 20″ line, measure out to right 8″. Place a square. Draw a line all the way across, from center to the square. Using a ruler, draw a slanted line joining the two squares. Two inches above the bottom line, draw a line across from the center to the outer edge. This will be the bottom portion of the bag. To the outer edge is added 1/4″ to 1/2″ seam allowance. Fold pattern in half lengthwise and cut out.

This one pattern serves a double purpose. First, the back of the bag and the flap are all in one. Because this is a reversible bag, cut *two outside fabrics* and only one interfacing (the reversible side will act as a lining) for each bag. Secondly, fold the flap portion to the back, out of the way, along the broken line. Then cut the front of the bag, adding a

Fig. 2–42 Reversible
bag: striped and quilted
calico patchwork.

seam allowance at the top above the broken line: Cut two outside fabrics and one interlining. If the bag is to be quilted, cut batting the same as the one interfacing.

ASSEMBLY

Step 1. Cut two straps, 30″ long x 2¹/₂″ wide, one from each fabric. Using 1″ washable
belt interfacing, make the strap using method one given earlier in this chapter. Leave
ends of strap raw (Fig. 2–1). Set aside.

Step 2. To support the weakest of the two outside fabrics, baste the one interlining to
it. If you're planning to quilt, slip the batting between the wrong side of the outside fabric
and the interlining. Trim off batting from seam allowance at flap section only. Quilt the
three pieces together for both the back and flap combination piece and the front. Even if

Fig. 2–43 Reversed calico bag shown in Fig. 2–42: solid color denim with emblem for decoration.

you're not planning to quilt, it is best to decoratively stitch the interlining to one of the outer pieces without batting. It will help to give the bag a better shape. *Step 3*. As the two combined back and flap pieces lay before you, you will note both have a dot and a square at the line between the back and the flap. Notch all four dots (Fig. 2–45a), using the square to indicate the side seam allowance.

Step 4. Position each set of bag fronts over their matching respective backs, right sides together, for both outside pieces. Stitch the sides and bottoms of the two separated shells (Fig. 2–45b). To square off the bottoms, pick up a corner and fold side seam against the bottom seam to form a point (see Fig. 2–22). Measure down 1¹/₂″ from the point and stitch straight across and back again for extra strength. Trim away excess point beyond stitching, leaving a ¹/₄″ seam. Repeat for the other three corners. Turn right-side-out and press. The side of the bag will have a wedge shape (Fig. 2–46).

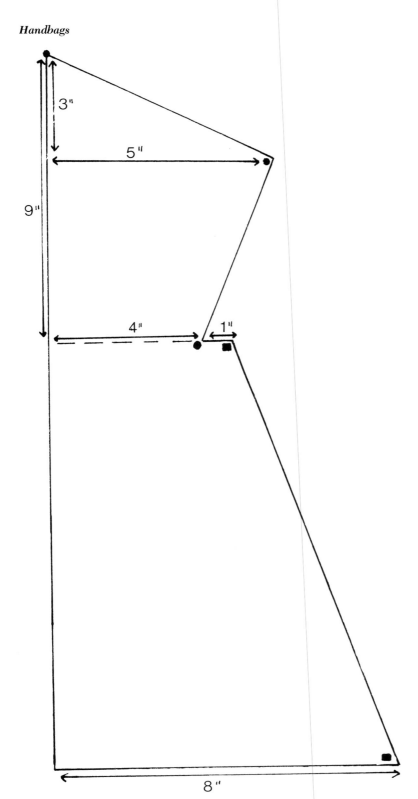

Fig. 2–44   Half the pattern for reversible bag.

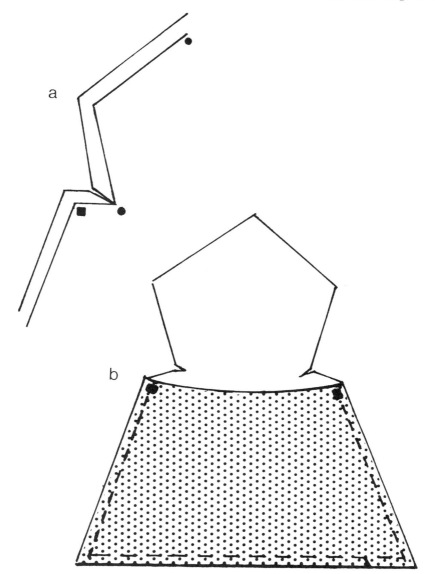

Fig. 2–45   a. Slash through seam allowance into the corner. b. Stitch front to back.

Step 5. Around the perimeter of the flap, the front openings of the two newly formed shells, turn the seam allowance to the wrong side, mitering the corners, then baste and press (Fig. 2–47). Turn the shell, without the interfacing attached, wrong-side-out and slip into the other shell, which is held right-side-out, adjusting the flap, front, and side opening to match. Slip in the raw end of the strap at the side front opening and baste the two shells together. Topstitch the shells around the perimeter, $1/8''$ from the two edges. For added strength, place a second row of top stitching $1/4''$ to $1/2''$ from the edge.

Step 6. If the bag is made of soft materials, then make a floorboard, approximately $13'' \times 2^{1}/4''$, to slip into the bag to hold the bottom firm.

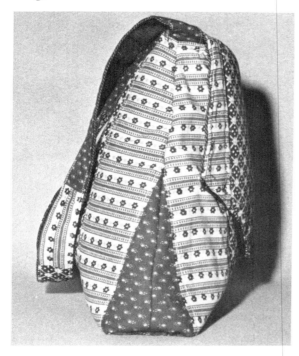

Fig. 2–46   Wedged side of bag.

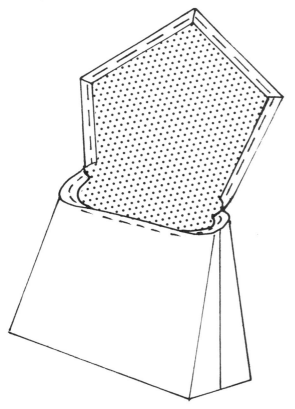

Fig. 2–47   Turn all raw-edge seam allowances to wrong side.

DOUBLE-POCKET ACCORDION BAG

This smart double-pocket bag is called an accordion because it has two separate pockets attached at the center. The styling accommodates almost any fabric suggested earlier and is quick to make. As shown in color Fig. 11, the red quilted washable wool with its long shoulder strap and novel button closure has a dressy appearance. The closure often sets the tone; a novelty suspender-strap closing on brushed denim is appropriate for school, while a frog closing on a tapestry could go to the theater. This bag can be made with square or round corners.

Work this bag step-by-step, reading carefully and holding materials as shown in the accompanying illustrations. This is not a beginner's styling. One needs a lot of experience making two or three other bags.

MATERIALS

$7/8$ yard of 45" outer fabric
$7/8$ yard of 45" lining
$1^1/4$ yards of 30" interlining
$1^1/2$ yards of 30" washable belt interlining for strap
14" of $1/4$" cording
decorative button
30" x 38" piece of batting (optional)

PREPARATION

Note: As you work, keep in mind that the first accordion pocket is formed by B1 and B3 and the second is formed by B2 and B4.

Cut two basic patterns for A and B, as shown in Fig. 2–48, seam allowances included. Using pattern piece B, cut *four* pieces from the outer fabric (label these pieces in pencil B1, B2, B3, B4). Cut four interlinings and four linings, and, if quilting, cut four pieces of batting. Using pattern piece A, cut one piece for the outer flap, one for the flap lining, one for the flap interlining, and, if quilting, one piece of batting, following Fig. 2–48 for layout suggestions. If you are using a lightweight fabric for the outer shell, then the flap lining may be cut from the outer fabric. However, if your outer fabric is heavy, then line the flap with the material used for lining the bag itself.

ASSEMBLY

Step 1. Prepare the two patch pockets for lining, no bigger than 5" x 5"; place one each in the center of two of the lining pieces. Place one lining piece with a pocket against a lining piece without a pocket, right sides together. Stitch a $1/2$" seam around the two sides and the bottom, starting and stopping $1/2$" from top of bag (Fig. 2–49a). Turn the opening on the top edges back to the wrong side $1/2$" and baste. Repeat procedure for the other two lining pieces and set aside.

Step 2. Prepare pieces B1, B2, B3, and B4 by placing the wrong side of each outer fabric against the interlining and basting $1/4$" around the edge; number each one in pencil on lining. If quilting is planned, the batting is added between the outer fabric and interlining. Baste and quilt with a diamond pattern on each of the four pieces (see Fig. 2–50).

Step 3. Place piece B1 (interlined fabric) down on the work surface, right-side-up. Place B2 on top, putting right sides together; the interlining sides face out and all edges should be matching. Pin the edges to hold B1 and B2 together.

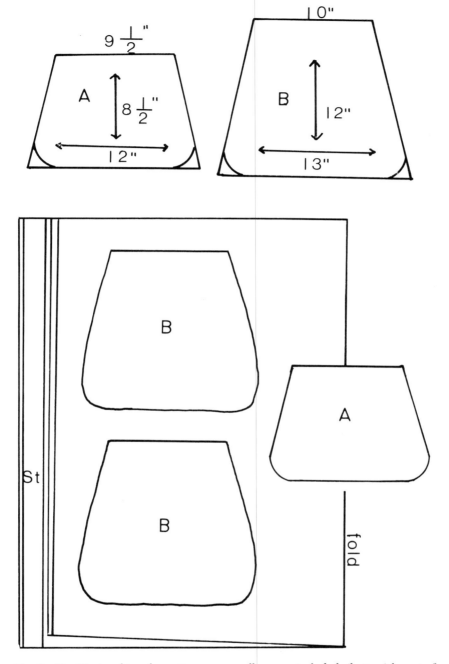

Fig. 2–48   *(Top)* making the patterns, seam allowance included; *(bottom)* layout of 45″ fabric for outer fabric. Note fold at right.

Step 4. With a pencil, draw a U-shaped line on the interlining 1¹/₂″ from the sides and 1¹/₂″ from the bottom. Beginning ¹/₂″ from top, stitch as shown in Fig. 2–49a. The top raw edge will remain open. Remove all pins.

Step 5. Fold the side and bottom edges of B2 in toward the center and hold with

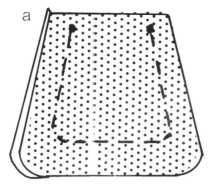
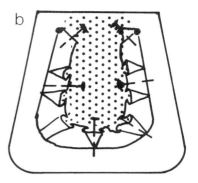

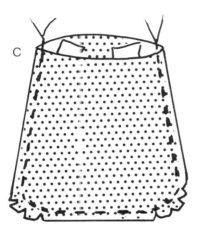

Fig. 2–49 Assembling the pockets a. Stitch the two inside pieces (B1 and B2) together. b. Fold edges of upper piece (B2) to center. c. Stitch two pieces (B1 and B3) to form first accordion pocket.

pins (Fig. 2–49*b*). Keep pinpoints buried in the interlining so they do not tear the fabric. The right side of piece B1 can now be seen around the folded edges of B2.

Step 6. Place B3 on top of this, with right side down and interlining up. Match all raw edges over the bulk of the B2 piece. Baste and sew 1/2″ from the edge on sides and bottom. Notch the rounded edges to release bulk at seams (Fig. 2–49*c*). Turn right-side-out and remove all pins. You have now formed *one* of the two accordion pockets.

Step 7. Turn the work completely over so that the outside of the newly formed accordion pocket (B1 and B3) faces up and the interlining of B2 is down on the work surface.

Step 8. Take both layers of the newly formed accordion pocket and fold side and bottom edges toward the center. Pin or baste toward the center, exposing the right side of B2 around the folded edges of the first accordion pocket (similar to Fig. 2–49*b*).

Step 9. Place B4 right-side-down over the folded-in accordion pocket, matching the raw edges and the right sides of B2 to B4. Pin the raw edges and stitch again, as in Fig. 2–49*c*, 1/2″ from the edge, beginning at the upper righthand corner. Notch the bottom corners and turn to the right side. Release all pins and the second accordion pocket is formed (Fig. 2–50).

Fig. 2–50   Closeup of quilting on the red wool accordion bag; view with two pockets open.

Step 10. Turn the upper raw edges of each of the two separate lower shells toward the inside ¹/₂″ and baste.

Step 11. Baste the inner sections of the two shells between points 1 and 2 (Fig. 2–51) Stitch permanently ¹/₄″ from the top edge. Press all edges lightly and set aside.

Step 12. To make the flap, place the interlining against the wrong side of the outside

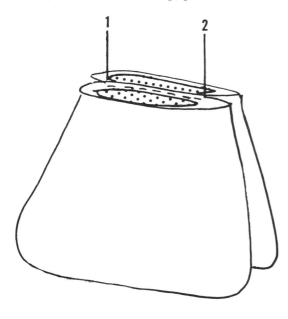

Fig. 2–51   Stitch the centers of the two lower shells together between points 1 and 2.

flap fabric. Baste the two pieces together ½″ from the edges, with a big X across the center. If quilting is planned, place the batting between the outside fabric and the interlining. Baste and quilt with a diamond pattern. When completed, treat as one piece.

Step 13. To make the button loop as shown, cut a piece of outside fabric 7″ long and 1½″ wide on the true bias. Cut a 14″ piece of ¼″ cording. Starting at one end of the cording, place fabric over the cording, right sides together. With the zipper foot of the machine placed against the bulk of the cording, sew with small stitches, stretching the bias as you form a fabric tube around the cording (Fig. 2–52). To secure cording to funnel, stitch across cording at center where outside fabric strip ends, as shown. Trim seam allowance to ¼″ to ⅛″ inch. This will leave about half of the cording uncovered.

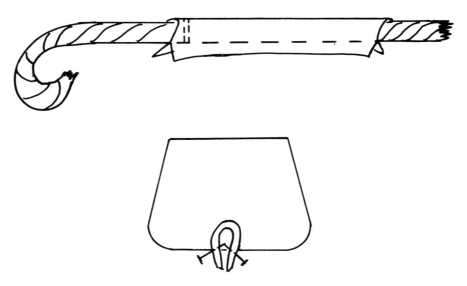

Fig. 2–52 (*Top*) making fabric-covered loop with cording filler; (*bottom*) placing loop on outside of flap.

Step 14. Pull the cording from the open end, working the funnel back over extended cord. When finished, the cording and the seam allowance will be on the inside. Measure the loop for the selected button, marking with two pins to indicate necessary length to go round the button. Add ¾″ at each end. Cut off excess.

Step 15. Trim out cording ½″ from each raw end beyond the pinpoints so *seam allowance and cording only remain in the center* (the part which will show on the outside of the bag). Pin upward on the exact center of the *outer flap*, placing the ends of the bias tube at the bottom edge of the flap (Fig. 2–52).

Step 16. Place the right side of the lining against the right side of outer fabric and sew ½″ all the way around the sides and across the bottom. Reinforce the loop closure area with extra stitches. Turn to the outside, then press on the lining side and set aside.

Step 17. Strap should be cut from outer fabric, 30″ x 3½″. Center the 1½″ belt interlining against the center of the wrong side of the outer fabric (see Fig. 2–1b). If a quilted bag is planned, then slip a 1½″ x 30″ piece of batting between the wrong side of outer fabric and belt interlining. Fold the left side of the strap to the back over the interlining, baste, and press. Turn the raw edge of the right side ¼″ toward the wrong side and then to the back, overlapping the basted left side, and baste down center. (If you use a selvage edge, then the ¼″ turnback need not be used.)

Fig. 2–53   Final assembly of flap and floral lining in each of the double-accordion pockets. Small stitches hold pockets together; large stitches hold lining to outer pockets.

Step 18. With the two accordion pockets before you, slip one pair of linings in each shell, wrong sides together, matching the folded-back edges of the top. Baste the lining to the front accordion pocket around the top edges.

Step 19. In the back portion of the second or back accordion pocket, place the strap ends 1″ from each outer edge. The straps will form a U shape. Then place the raw edge of the flap. Baste the lining to the back accordion pocket, catching the flap, the straps, and back of the bag (Fig. 2–53).

Step 20. Stitch permanently, 1/4″ from the folded edge around the top of each of the separate shells (except at the center where the two pockets were already joined). Press lightly and sew button in place. Press permanently.

FAKE FUR BAG

A fake fur bag is one of the most stunning of all winter accessories (Fig. 2–54). It doubles its value if matched up with a fake fur hat (see color Figs. 1 and 9). Special attention has been given to the pattern, making sure the pile of the fur runs in the downward direction. The fur is further enhanced by the use of a metal chain. This bag can be repeated in fabric, too, but would need the strength of an interlining. It is not a beginner's style but could be a success after working out two or three of the other bags in this book. Reread the information on fake fur in Chapter One and pretest the fur that you purchase before getting started.

Fig. 2–54   Long-pile white fake fur bag with double-link gold chain.

MATERIALS

    outer fabric: $^1/_2$ yard of 60″
    interlining: 1 yard of 30″ (optional)
    lining: $^3/_4$ yard of 45″
    chain for handle: 4 feet

PREPARATION

    Make the front and back pattern on large graph paper (18″ x 22″), using Fig. 2–55 as a guide. Fold the paper in half lengthwise. About an inch from the top, place a vertical line 10″ long, along the fold. Starting from the top of the vertical line, measure out 7″, draw a solid line to the right at the end, and place a little *x*. Measure down 8″ from the top of the line and place a dot on the center line. On the newly made dot, measure out 8″ to the right and mark with an *x*. At the bottom of the center line, measure out to the right 6″ and draw a solid line at the end, then place an *x*. Connect the three *x*s with shallow curved lines, as shown. This represents half the bag. Add the seam allowance. Note the grain line for the fur on the pattern, fur should run down in the direction of the arrows.

    To make the pattern for the flap, draw a vertical line on the center fold 9″ long (Fig. 2–55). At the top of the line, draw a horizontal line out to the right 6″, place an *x* at the end of the line. Working from the top, measure down 2″ on the center line. Place a dot

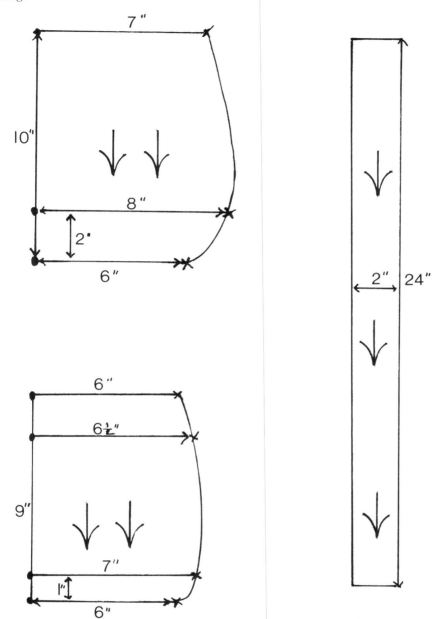

Fig. 2–55 Half-pattern for fake fur bag: arrows indicate direction of fur. Add seam allowance.

and measure out to the right horizontally 6½". Place an x. From the top of the line measure down 8" and place a dot on the center line. From the dot, measure out 7" and place an x. At the bottom of the vertical line, place a horizontal line 6" long and place an x at the end of the line. Connect the xs with a shallow curved line. This is half the flap—add seam allowance, fold paper in half, and cut out. This is the pattern for the flap. Note the direction of the fur. The flap will be narrower than the front and back of the bag. This is to allow for easy opening of the back and less wear on the pile of the fur.

Draw a rectangle 24″ long by 2″ wide. This will be the side panel pattern for the bag. Note the direction of the fur.

Cut one back and one front from the fake fur; using the same pattern, cut two lining pieces. (No interlining is needed unless working with very soft fur or interpreting this styling in regular fabric.) Cut one flap from the fake fur and one from the lining material. Cut two side panels from the fake fur with the fur going in the same direction on both. Insert a small safety pin on the wrong side of each piece to indicate the direction of the fur. Cut two lining pieces to match.

ASSEMBLY

Step 1. Attach the two side panel pieces together so long pile meets at the center seam.

Step 2. Select one piece for the back of the bag, fold in half crosswise, and mark center with a pencil on the back. Place the center seam of the side panels against the center back, right sides together. Pin and baste the side panels to the back, moving up the two sides. You will note that a good portion of the ends of the side panels extend above the top of the bag. Baste, then stitch permanently. Stop the stitching at the seam allowance, not through it, at the top of the bag (Fig. 2–56). After sewing, notch and trim excess fiber from the seams. Repeat for the placing of the front piece to the side panels (Fig. 2–56). Turn bag right-side-out.

Step 3. Make the flap by placing the right side of the lining against the right side of the outside fabric. Stitch around the sides and the bottom. Leave the 12″ top open. Turn to the right side and press lightly on the lining side. Center the flap against the back of the bag with right sides together and baste in place. The sides of the flap will not be as big as the back of the bag (Fig. 2–57).

Step 4. To make the lining for lower half of the bag, start by placing a patch pocket, 7″ x 8″, against the back of the bag lining. Following the instructions in step 2, make the lining the same as the outside of the bag, but leave a *10″ opening in the seam* at the bottom of the front of the lining (see Fig. 2–13). Slip the right side of the lining up against the right side of the bag (over the flap that has been attached to the back). Baste and stitch permanently *across the front and the back only*. Do not cross the side panels at all. After stitching, pull the outer shell of the bag through the opening in the bottom of the lining (see Figs. 2–13 and 2–14). Place the lining in the bag and slipstitch the opening in the lining closed.

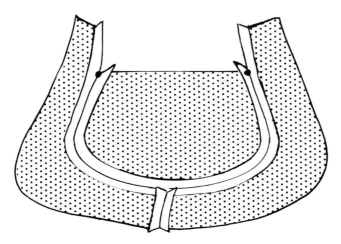

Fig. 2–56   Setting the sides into the front.

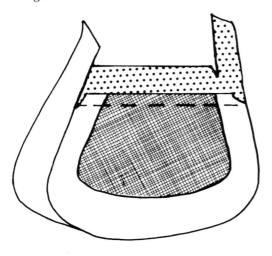

Fig. 2–57   Setting the flap against the back.

Step 5. Turn the three remaining edges of the ends of the fur side panels to the wrong side and baste. Do the same for the matching lining piece (Fig. 2–58). Place the lining against the fake fur and, using a rather long needle, hand slipstitch together with small stitches. Fold this tab against the lining, forming a loop (Fig. 2–58). Stitch down permanently by hand, stitching the end of the loop to the lining and the wrong side of the outside fabric. (For such bulky projects, a long needle such as a milliner's needle or a darning needle is recommended.)

Step 6. Insert chain through the two loops, forming one long circle of chain (Fig. 2–59). Open one of the end links of the chain and secure it to the other end. This bag was planned as a shoulder bag; however, it would look equally good with a short handle. Use the wrong end of a long heavy needle to pull all fur pile from seams and vacuum any loose fiber from the bag before you use it.

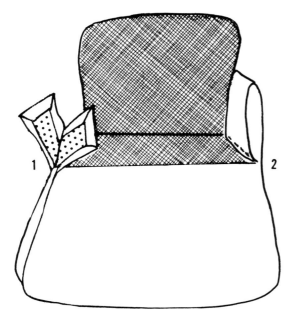

Fig. 2–58   Form the loop for the chain, using the lining and the outer fabric (*left*). *At right,* folding loops back against the inside.

Fig. 2–59   Looking down into the fake fur bag. Chain looped through folded tabs at side of bag.

BEACHMAT AND BAG COMBINATION

This novelty item serves two purposes. First, it is a beach mat. When you go to or from the beach or pool, it zips into a tote to carry sun gear. (See color Fig. 10, floral chintz bag with its open-crown brimmer to match.) The sides have set-in separating zippers and it sports a narrow handle. For added softness and quick drying, it is suggested that a polyester filling be used. Terrycloth would be a good substitute. The lining may or may not be of the same fabric. Our print bag sports a check lining (Fig. 2–60).

MATERIALS

    72″ x 29″ outside fabric, rather sturdy
    60″ x 29″ lining (it could be the same as outside, or contrast, or terrycloth)
    60″ x 29″ interlining (it could be cotton or polyester batting, or terrycloth)
    1″ wide x 60″ long washable belt interlining
    two 14″ separating zippers

PREPARATION

The pattern for outside fabric is 60″ x 29″. Cut one piece for outside 60″ x 29″, one lining, and one batting (or terrycloth) interlining. Cut two strap pieces 2″ x 29″. Cut eight pieces 2″ x $14\frac{1}{2}$″ for zip tab holders.

Step 1. Fold the outside and lining fabrics in half crosswise, then in half again, making four quarters (Fig. 2–61a). Press. This will give a point of reference. Fold the sixteen narrow ends of the side zip tabs $\frac{1}{4}$″ to the wrong side of the fabric, on all eight pieces.

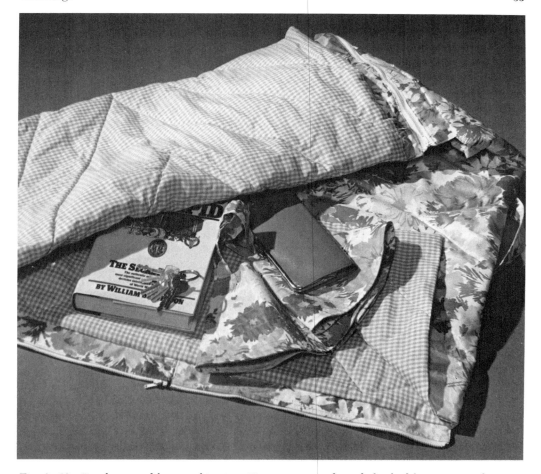

Fig. 2–60 Beachmat and bag combination. Note print outside and checked lining. Note that zipside is closed at top of photo and open across bottom. Hat folded inside is the sunbrimmer (see Fig. 5–9).

Step 2. Place the edge of the zipper against the right side edges of one side tab. Baste in place. Place a second tab on top, right sides together. Sew three layers together with zipper foot ¼″ in from the edge (Fig. 2–61b). Open away from zipper, placing wrong sides together (Fig. 2–61c). Press and baste. Topstitch ⅛″ from the edge, along top, zipper tape, and bottom. Repeat for the other half of the zipper. Then repeat this procedure for the second zipper. Set aside.

Step 3. Open zipper tabs to make four pieces. Baste into place along each side of the lower portion of the outside fabric. The bottom of each zipper tape must meet at the center fold line. Be sure you have one zipper top and its matching mate on one side. Use Fig. 2–61d as a guide.

Step 4. On a large work surface, place the 60″ x 29″ batting; on top, with the wrong side against batting, place the outside fabric. On top of this place the lining fabric, right sides together with outside fabric. Baste ½″ off the raw edge. Leave a 12″ opening at the top. Stitch permanently and turn right-side-out, pulling very gently through the opening at the top. Trim batting back at opening and slipstitch the lining and outside fabric to close the opening.

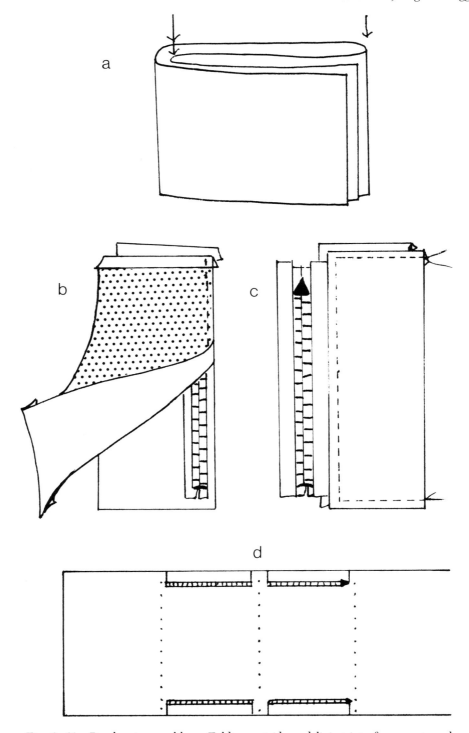

Fig. 2–61   Beachmat assembly a. Folding outside and lining into four quarters. b and c. Making zipper tabs. d. Placing zipper tabs against outside fabric.

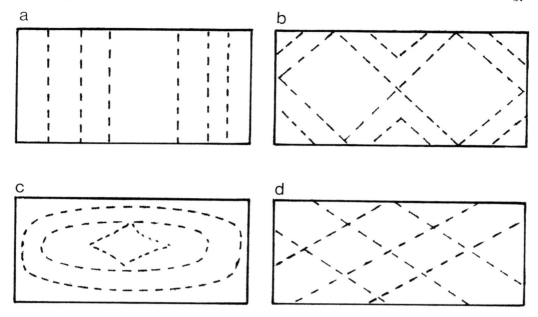

Fig. 2–62 Quilt designs. a. Pipelines. b. Large geometric. c. Ovals. d. Diamonds.

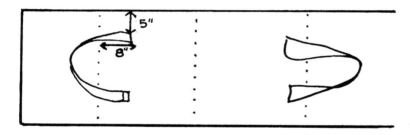

Fig. 2–63 Place-
ment of straps.

Step 5. Because the batting can tear and break from excessive wear, place a few lines of quilting stitches across to firm up the three layers. See Fig. 2–62 for suggestions.

Step 6. Make the straps, using method two (Fig. 2–1). Interline straps if fabric is thin. Leave the ends raw so they may be turned to the wrong side. Place the straps in position on the outside fabric, using Fig. 2–63 as a guide. Turn under the ends, pin, and baste through all layers. Stitch permanently through all layers about 5″ up both sides of the strap from the bottom.

Step 7. To fold: Fold each end a quarter toward the inside, fold in half again, and zip up the sides (see Fig. 2–60). Fill bag with favorite sunshine gear and hop off to the beach, pool, or picnic. Remember that the outside fabric should be placed against the sand or chair—not the lining.

3

Junior Bags

This is a special section set aside for the beginner in needlecrafts. The experience of making something both useful and attractive when young can be the key to a long lifetime of sewing. The projects shown here can be made as beginner classroom projects, extra-credit projects, or to fill in a few days at the end of a school year. They can be planned as youth group and Scout projects, for the girls to use for themselves, as gifts, or for resale.

Pay close attention to the fabrics suggested and additional information given to help make the projects a success. Make the patterns for the second two bags on brown super-market-bag paper that has been pressed to remove the creases. The patterns are different and this will give you a chance to test your accuracy in measuring and tracing.

After this beginning, the young seamstress may like to try the biscuit bag or another of the simple bags in Chapter Two. Hats are fun to make and the young person may enjoy making the open-crown hats.

REVERSIBLE HOBO

This sack, with its easy shoulder carry tie, is just right for the youngster on the go. Its expandable styling packs everything—from a few books to lunch for the "troops." It is most important that two layers of tightly woven broadcloth be used, one for the outside and one for the lining. It is possible to reverse this bag, so choose colors that coordinate well with clothing. (See the hobo in color, Fig. 4, made in dark blue paisley lined with a multicolor patchwork print, and in Fig. 3–1.)

MATERIALS

> two 36″ squares of tightly woven broadcloth (you may have to take 1 yard of each at
>   45″ and cut down)
> one 16″ separating zipper, metal preferred

PREPARATION

This bag can be made by hand, using a needle marked "sharp," about $1^{1}/_{2}$″ to $1^{3}/_{4}$″ in length. Stitch with a backstitch. It can be worked on the sewing machine with a regular #11 or #14 needle and regular dressmaker thread. Cut two 36″ squares from each fabric.

Fig. 3–1 Reversible hobo bag
made of printed broadcloth.

ASSEMBLY

Step 1. Place the squares on top of each other, with right sides (show-off sides) together.

Step 2. Use Fig. 3–2*a* as a guide: Measure in 10″ from opposite corners and cut across only those two corners. Pencil in seam allowance ¼″ from raw edge all around.

Step 3. Use Fig. 3–2*b* as a guide. Baste first, then stitch as indicated. Note that you will stop stitching ¼″ from the edge. Turn to the outside (right side). *Press* all stitched edges. Stay at the ironing board and fold the raw edges of the two openings to the inside. First pin, then press, making sure to get the seam allowance pressed in nicely.

Baste each edge back separately so you have a nice opening, like an envelope opening. Find the center of the opening by folding in half or use a ruler. Make a pencil dot on the folded-in portion. Open the zipper and press edge tapes flat so they are easy to handle. Press the ends of tapes back out of the way. You cannot hold these ends with your fingers, so place a pin with a *metal head* right into the soft top of the ironing board to hold the folded-back top edges (Fig. 3–2*c*). Press on top with point of iron. Wait a few minutes before taking out the hot pins. Fold the zipper in half and put a pencil dot at its center on both sides of the metal zipper. Look at the zipper. See that there is a top end with a pull tab and a bottom end.

Step 4. Open the zipper so you have two separate pieces. Use Fig. 3–2*d* as a guide: Place one piece in one of the opening edges. The fold of the edge will be close to the metal teeth of the zipper. Match the dot on zipper with dot on the fold. This will help you get the zipper centered. Be careful to place top at one end of opening. With small basting stitches about ½″ long, baste the zipper into opening, stitching through the two layers of fabric with the zipper tape between. Repeat with the other half of zipper in the other side opening, as shown.

After basting, to check your work for accuracy, fold in half. Put zippers together (Fig. 3–2*e*). If any adjustments have to be made, it is easy to open up the basting stitches and

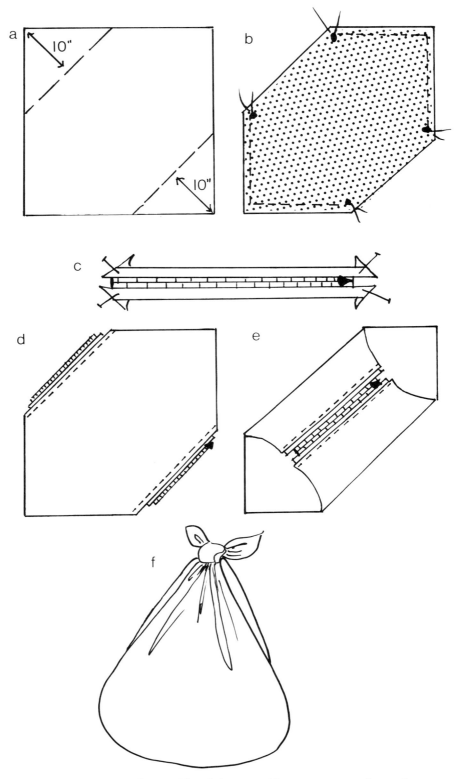

Fig. 3–2 Cutting and assembling hobo. a. Fold square on true diagonal. Measure 10″ from opposite corners, along diagonal fold. Cut off corners along broken lines. b. Stitch on wrong side. Stop stitching at large dots. c. Turn ends of zipper back, pin to ironing board, and press. d. Slip each half of zipper into opening and topstitch closed. e. Fold in half, closing zipper. f. Tie knot in remaining ends.

readjust now. Open article flat to sew zipper permanently with a backstitch by hand or on the machine—but stay close to the edge (Fig. 3–2*d*).

Step 5. Close zipper. (Fig. 3–2*e*). Draw up the two remaining ends and tie (Fig. 3–2*f*). Sling over the shoulder. You're ready to go. It is best never to take the tie out of the top: Open the zipper to get in and out.

ROPE RINGER

This is a soft, casual version of a more formal bag done on rigid rings. It is a soft, pouchie bag made to be worn high on the shoulder (Fig. 3–3). It has to be made from heavy denim, canvas, drill, or very heavy material that has edges that will not ravel because it has no lining. The straps can be rope (from a hardware store), foldover braid, heavy leather strapping, such as leather shoelaces (shoe repair shop), macrame ropes done in a fancy design, or link chain.

If you are going to braid or knot your strap material, you will need about one and a half times the amount suggested in the materials list, because braiding and knotting reduces the length to some degree. The bag in Fig. 3–3 has pressed-on initials cut from Bondex, a self-adhesive material used for patching clothing. They were cut out and ironed onto the front of the bag after the bag was finished. It can hold school or team emblems, or be made in a light color so friends can sign it with an indelible laundry marker. It stands alone without trimmings, too.

MATERIALS

    1 yard of heavy fabric, such as denim, canvas, drill, or duck

    2 yards of rope, 1/2″ diameter

    one spool of heavy-duty thread to match bag (not extra strong used for buttons or carpet sewing)

    one #18 machine needle

Fig. 3–3 Rope Ringer made of drill, signed with indelible marker and monogrammed.

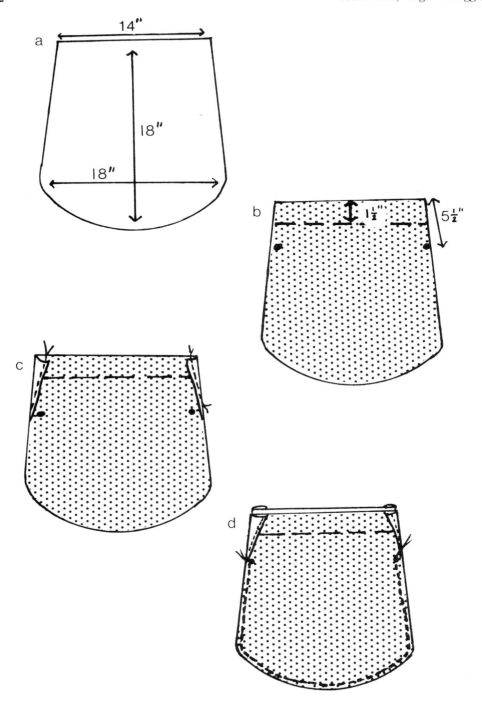

Fig. 3–4   a. Pattern includes ¹/₂″ seam allowance. The shape of the bottom of the bag is optional; it can be squared off, too. b. Place marks on wrong side of bag. c. Fold in side tops of bag to form a wedge. d. Place two pieces together, stitch across the end of folds on an angle over bottom stitches of wedge. Continue, forming a ¹/₂″ seam around raw edge (see also Fig. 2–20).

PREPARATION

Put the #18 needle on your machine and thread with heavy-duty thread. Set the stitch guide so that you get eight to ten stitches to an inch.

ASSEMBLY

Step 1. Make a pattern from paper, using Fig. 3–4*a* as a guide.

Step 2. On the *wrong* side of the fabric, pin the pattern. Try to place the top of the bag against the selvage, if possible. Draw the pattern with regular lead pencil. Do the same for the second piece and cut out on pencil line. On the wrong side, measure down 1½″ from the top and mark with a little dash. Along this line, place a row of ½″-long basting stitches on both pieces of the bag. On the wrong side at the sides of the bag, measure down 5½″ from the top and place a dot (Fig. 3–4*b*). Measure in ½″ at the top. Fold edge at the top to the wrong side ½″ and continue to fold, shaping fold to nothing, like a wedge. Stitch by hand, using a running stitch, or by machine permanently, holding these folds to the back. Repeat for the second piece (Fig. 3–4*c*).

Step 3. Place the two pieces together with outsides (or right sides) touching and baste. Seam the two together. Start stitching at point of V, backstitching to reinforce. Make seam ½″ deep (Fig. 3–4*d*). Stitch around a second time for reinforcement or use zigzag foot over edges, if you have one. Set aside.

Step 4. Cut length of rope in half and slightly fray the four ends to flatten. Form a circle with one rope. Bring ends together and center the ends against the wrong side, above the basted line on one piece (Fig. 3–5*a*). Stitch edges securely to center, preferably by machine. Do not allow stitching to extend below the basted line. Carefully fold back the top of the bag so the fold appears on the basting line, trapping the rope inside. Baste raw edge against the inside of bag and stitch permanently ¼″ off the edge. If fabric will ravel easily, then fold the edge in ¼″ to the wrong side and stitch close to the edge

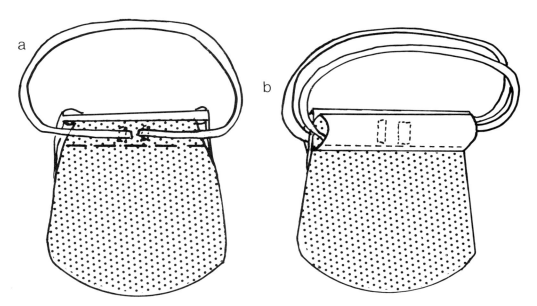

Fig. 3–5 Adding rope straps a. Pin back one top against itself. Loop rope around in circle, placing both frayed ends at the center, above basting. b. Fold 1½″ top to the wrong side and topstitch the tunnel closed.

(Fig. 3–5*b*). Repeat for the other side. Turn to the right side and gently gather the sides toward the center of the rope, forming a pouchie little bag.

An alternate way to do the strap is to turn the top down to the wrong side and stitch, forming a tunnel, then work through a soft strap material, such as leather strips (shoelaces) and tie at the top.

Apply the iron-on trim. If you wish to use your embroidery skills, then apply stitches or trim before the bag is put together.

DOUBLE-POCKET MINI BAG

The newest little bag, to wear straight from the shoulder or belted around the waist, is a good complement for every outfit. The fabric must be very sturdy, such as canvas, denim, drill, duck, or drapery material. The edging on the one shown in Fig. 3–6 and color Fig. 4 is purchased bias binding. It should be ³/₄″ to 1″ wide, not counting the folded-back edges. The binding should be in a contrasting color. This is best worked on the sewing machine.

MATERIALS

¹/₂ yard of sturdy outside fabric (canvas is the vogue now)
3 yards of bias binding
one button, 1″ wide

PREPARATION

Use a #14 needle in your machine and heavy-duty thread matching the binding color. Copy the four pattern pieces in Figs. 3–7 and 3–8. Use Fig. 3–7 to cut three pattern pieces and Fig. 3–8 for the flap. Trace patterns on brown supermarket-bag paper. The patterns are only half size and you must enlarge to full width by placing on a fold of paper. Cut out the four pieces, marking the top flat edge of bag with number from each pattern. Number each piece as indicated.

Fig. 3–6   Double-pocket mini bag, made of canvas and trimmed with bias binding.

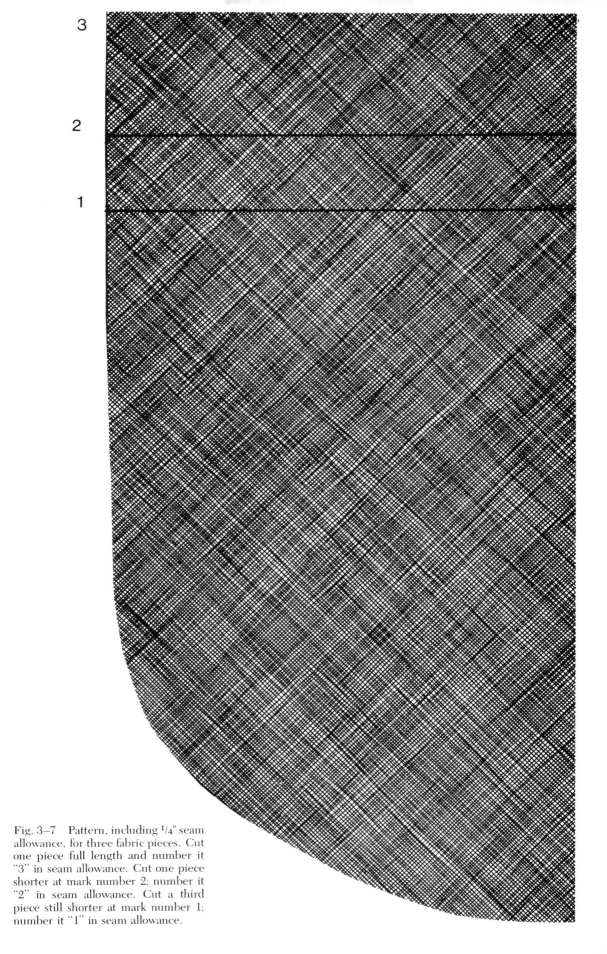

3

2

1

Fig. 3–7 Pattern, including ¼″ seam
allowance, for three fabric pieces. Cut
one piece full length and number it
"3" in seam allowance. Cut one piece
shorter at mark number 2; number it
"2" in seam allowance. Cut a third
piece still shorter at mark number 1;
number it "1" in seam allowance.

Flap

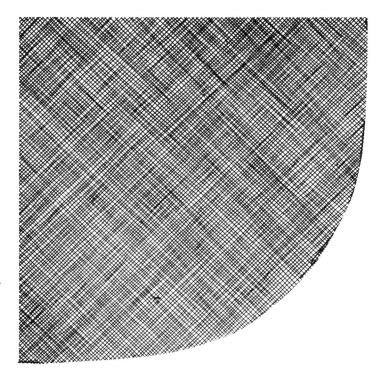

Fig. 3–8 Pattern, including ¼″ seam allowance, for flap. Cut one. Underneath is a small diagram of how the pieces should look with their respective numbers.

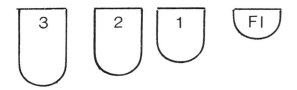

ASSEMBLY

Step 1. To make the closure loop, cut off 4″ of bias binding. Fold in half lengthwise and stitch the length together with wrong sides together. Fold in half to find the middle and place a pin at the center. Using Fig. 3–9*a* as a guide, fold up one side, press, and pin. Fold up the remaining side, making edges that meet in the center touch. Take out center pin (Fig. 3–9*b*). Press and pin remaining fold. Stitch across bottom to hold diagonal folds in place, along the dotted line. Stitch across dotted line at top near the edge to hold top together. The front side is shown. Place the *wrong* side of the loop against the *wrong* side of the front flap and stitch edge. Keep this loop positioned with safety pin until after the next step (Fig. 3–10*a*).

Step 2. Fold the remaining binding in half, wrong sides together, and press. Sometimes this binding can be purchased prefolded. If so, omit this pressing step. Cut a piece

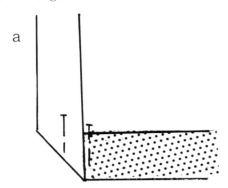

a

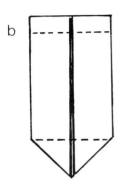

b

Fig. 3–9   Making a loop closure, using bias binding *folded in half* a. Cut a length of binding, divide in half, mark with a pin and fold one side
back, forming a 45-degree angle. b. Repeat for the
other side and stitch across on top and bottom to
hold folds.

of folded binding 14″ long. Place around the raw edge of the round portion of the flap.
Baste in place, catching both front and back edges. Pass binding right over the ends of
loop made before. Sew permanently with one row of stitches.

Step 3. Flip the loop downward and sew in place with a few machine stitches. Trim
raw edges of the bias even with the fabric. Center the newly made flap on top of piece 2.
Baste a piece of $8^1/4$″-long double-fold bias binding across the top, covering the raw edge
of the top of the flap *and* the raw edge of the top of piece 2 together under the bias binding (Fig. 3–10*b*). Sew permanently right at edge.

Step 4. Place $8^1/4$″ of bias binding across the flat top of piece 1 and place $8^1/4$″ of bias
binding across the top of piece 3. Sew permanently. Trim all edges.

Step 5. Lay piece 3 on the work surface before you, right-side-up. Onto this piece
place piece 2, with its flap attached (Fig. 3–10*c*). Place this piece so it is a little below the
flat top and the rounded sides and bottom are even. Turn the flap upward and place the
last remaining piece 1 on top of the other two, sides and bottom matching (Fig. 3–10*d*).
Place flap in a downward position. Baste all three layers together no deeper than $1/2$″ off
the edges.

Step 6. Fold remaining binding in half lengthwise, find the center, and place at the
bottom of the triple-layered bag. Pin, then baste remaining binding up the sides. Continue the binding off the top of the bag, forming straps. Sew permanently, keeping
stitching close to the edge. Tie small knots in each end of the straps, then square knot the
two straps together. Place button in right position to be caught by the buttonhole loop.

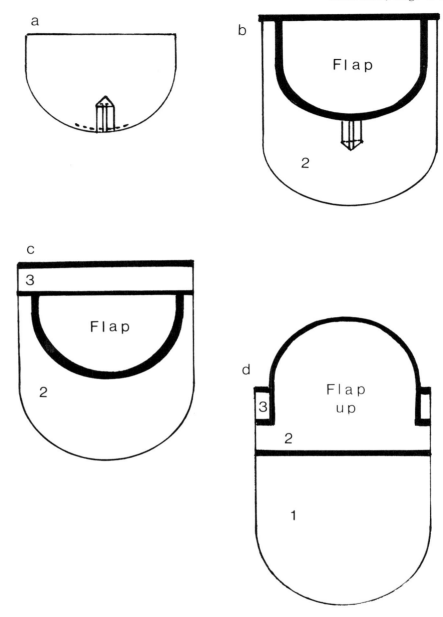

Fig. 3–10   Assembling the double-pocket bag a. Center the wrong side of bottom loop's raw edges against the raw edge of the wrong side of the flap. b. Place bound flap against piece 2. Bind the flat top of flap and piece 2 together. c. Place the combined flap and piece 2 on top of piece 3, which has its flat top bound. d. Lift flap upward and place piece 1 on top of the other two pieces, all round bottom edges together. Flat top edges will be staggered.

4
Nomad Travel Luggage

Today people travel with ease and in casual attire. Luggage for today must be suitable for business trips, weekend or weeklong vacations, trips to schools, boating, or backpacking. The key requirements of luggage are versatility and flexibility. The nomad styles planned here provide a unique combination of smart good looks, maximum strength, and minimum weight. They wear well and weigh little because they are fashioned of today's serviceable fabrics (see color Figs. 3 and 5). One of the wonderful things about the nomad styles is that many sizes are suggested, as well as many variations. This offers a springboard for new ideas.

Featured here are two styles of *braid-trimmed canvas totes* in different sizes, one featuring the zip-top wallet pocket inside; the *soft suitcase* in the flight bag size, or in the overnight attache size, or as a large handbag; the *chunky duffle*, supported on smart luggage webbing straps; the universally beloved *backpack* for the young at heart; the newest invention—the hang-up *suit bag*—and the longer, wider *dress bag* that holds three garments.

The best fabrics to scout up are the hardest wearing ones, such as canvas, real pants denim, upholstery, and tapestry of the upholstery classification. They need no additional backing. The new suede-finish fabrics, drapery fabrics, and corduroy made for slipcovers and draperies can be used very successfully. For long service it might be best to use a lining of drill or real pillow ticking as a backing. Cut the linings the same size as the outer pieces, baste to the outer pieces, and treat as a unit, except where the straps are lined with strong belt interlinings.

To save time and space, we have used the directions given in the beginning of Chapter Two for the various methods of making straps, floorboards, pockets, and seams. To work in this section, use heavy-duty thread and a #18 machine needle. You will note that most of the styles have been made in canvas. The reason canvas is so serviceable is that it is one of the few fabrics made that is waterproof.

TRIPLE-POCKET JIFFY SHOPPER

This bag is for shopping, school, or travel, and has two large, obvious pockets and one hidden pocket. Use fabric that is sturdy and can take a lot of wear, such as canvas, drill, denim, upholstery, or heavy drapery fabric. Two sizes are given: smaller 15″ x 15″ and larger 18″ x 18″. (See color Fig. 3 and Fig. 4–1.)

MATERIALS

> outside canvas, 30″ wide: 1 yard for small; 1¹/₂ yards for large
> bias-fold braid: 4¹/₂ yards for small; 6 yards for large
> 1″ wide x 40″ long washable belt interlining
> 6″ wide strip of matching color Velcro
> optional assorted trims

PREPARATION

Seam allowances are included in the pattern (Fig. 4–2). Cut four squares, 15″ x 15″ (or for larger bag, 18″ x 18″). Lay them one on top of the other, with the top one wrong-side-up on the pile. Draw or fold two diagonal lines across the wrong side of the top piece. Round the bottom corners to a depth of 1″, as shown in Fig. 4–2a. Cut a dart, centered on the diagonal line, 2¹/₂″ deep by ¹/₂″ wide at the bottom (Fig. 4–2a). Cut two 20″ straps, 3″ wide.

Fig. 4–1   (*From left*) canvas carryall, triple-pocket jiffy shopper, and duffle bag.

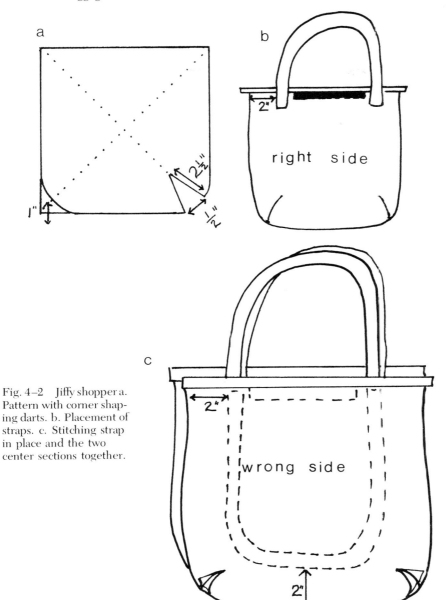

Fig. 4–2 Jiffy shopper a. Pattern with corner shaping darts. b. Placement of straps. c. Stitching strap in place and the two center sections together.

ASSEMBLY

Step 1. Make straps, using strap method two, Fig. 2–1. Reinforce with extra stitching.

Step 2. Across each top, or flat 15″ end, cover with braid, allowing an inch to stick out on either end.

Step 3. The V-shaped slashes in the bottom are to be sewn closed to the wrong side, just as a dart. Try to make the darts rounded. On the seam allowance of the dart, reinforce with two more rows of stitches. There will be eight darts in all.

Step 4. Separate the 6″ piece of Velcro. Center each piece just below the binding on the right side of two separate pieces of the four large pieces. Stitch around the edges, securing the Velcro to the fabric. Close the Velcro, making the two pieces adhere to each other, and make sure you have them centered exactly. Open the two pieces and lay them flat before you on the table, right-side-up. Place the straps 2″ in from the sides in a U-shaped position, close to the edges of the Velcro (Fig. 4–2b). Baste into place. Place the two pieces together, making the Velcro adhere. Sew two rows of stitches 1″ apart, around in a U shape, catching the edges of the strap and across the top of each strap as indicated in Fig. 4–2c. This forms a private pocket that can hold very personal articles (mad money).

Step 5. Pin the edges of one of the sides to the center, as in Fig. 2–49b. Trim the excess braid from the ends of the top. Place one of the remaining pieces over the un-pinned side, wrong sides together, and pin a piece of 47″ braid around the outside on top, tucking the 1″ excess at the top to the wrong side. This forms the second pocket.

Step 6. Release the pins, holding the third pocket out of the way. Place the last piece over the remaining wrong side to form the last pocket, following step 5.

CANVAS CARRYALL

This quick-to-make traveler is presented in two sizes: 10″ x 12″ x 6″ with 8″ high handles; 18″ x 20′ x 6″ with 5″ high handles. It has no lining and easy outside seams covered in double-fold braid. It has the optional feature of a zip-open wallet pocket.

Canvas is an ideal handbag fabric. It comes in many bright and serviceable colors and has no right or wrong side. Canvas is water repellent and therefore makes an ideal beach or book bag. (See color Fig. 5 and Fig. 4–1.) There are a few fabrics that can be substituted for canvas: real blue-jean *denim, tapestry, suede cloth,* heavily *quilted material,* real *sailcloth,* or sporty looking *upholstery* fabric.

Instructions are given for the small size, with the larger dimensions in parentheses.

MATERIALS

> 7/8 yards (1 1/4 yards) of 30″ canvas
> 2 1/2 yards (3 1/4 yards) of woven double-fold braid (1″ wide when open)
> 84″ of 1 1/2″ wide (3 yards of 2″ wide) embroidered cotton braid
> 1 1/2 yards of 1 1/2″ wide (1 yard of 2″ wide) washable belt interlining
> 7″ neckline zipper for pocket (*optional*)

PREPARATION

Using the pattern layout in Fig. 4–3 as a guide, cut the following pieces: one front and one back, 13″ x 15″ (21″ x 23″); two sides, 6″ x 12 1/2″ (7″ x 19 1/2″); two strap linings, 2″ x 20″ (2 1/2″ x 15″); two wallet pockets, 6 1/2″ x 8″; one piece of interlining for the strap, 2″ x 20″ (2 1/2″ x 15″). Seam allowances are included.

ASSEMBLY

Step 1. Begin assembly of this bag with its optional feature, the wallet pocket. If you don't want the pocket, then skip to step 3. Hold one side of the wallet pocket in front of you. Measure down 1 1/2″ from the top of one long 8″ side. Mark and cut on line. Fold back 1/4″ the two edges which were just cut, then press. Center the folded edges on either side of the zipper tapes and stitch down, using zipper foot (Fig. 4–4a). This is now the front of the wallet pocket.

Step 2. Place zippered front side against the back, wrongsides together. Trim the bottom corners into curves. Place the double-fold binding over raw edge, starting at point R, all the way around the bottom of the pocket to point L. Place pins across the binding

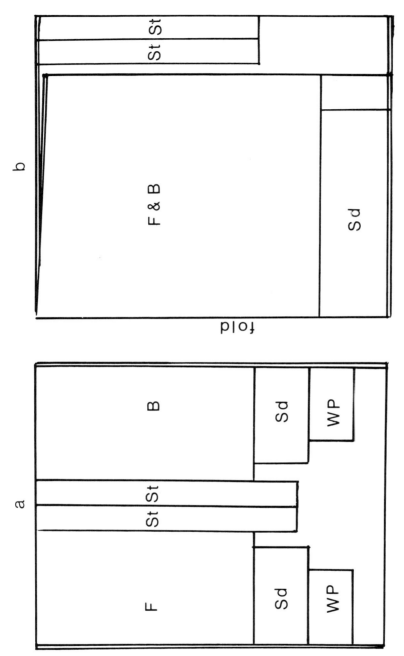

Fig. 4–3 Layouts for carryalls a. Small size bag: lay fabric open on work surface. b. Large size bag: fold fabric over and back against self 19".

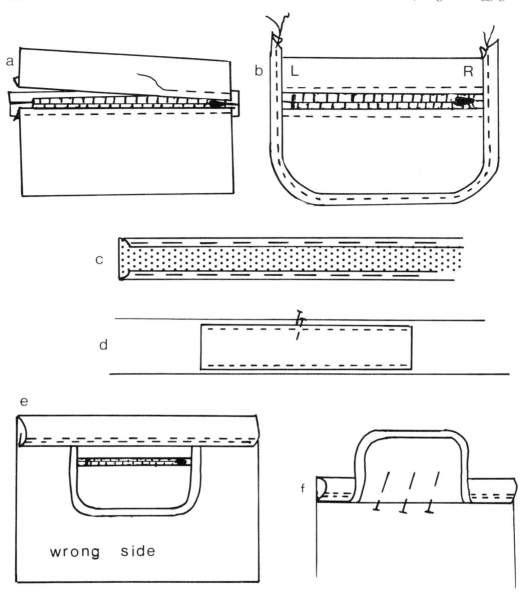

Fig. 4–4 Carryall assembly a. Putting zipper into front of wallet pocket. b. Finishing wallet pocket with double-fold braid. c. Placing interlining in strap lining. d. Centering strap lining against wrong side of outer strap. e. Placing wallet pocket in position. f. Pinning wallet pocket out of the way.

to hold in place while sewing. Stitch with matching colored thread $^1/_8''$ from edge of the binding (Fig. 4–4*b*). Run a row of machine stitches across the top, $^1/_4''$ from the raw edge, and set wallet pocket aside.

    Step 3. Fold in $^1/_4''$ from raw edge on long side of canvas strap lining for strap 20″ x 2″ (15″ x 2$^1/_2$″), reducing the strap to 20″ x 1$^1/_2$″ (15″ x 2″). Slip the washable belt interlining under the $^1/_4''$ folded edges. The other two ends are left raw. Baste down folded edges securely over belt interlining (Fig. 4–4*c*). Mark the middle of the long strap with a pin set in at a right angle. Repeat for the second strap lining.

Step 4. Cut off two lengths of embroidered ribbon trim, 42″ (54″) long. Find the middle and mark with a pin set in at a right angle. Place one piece of the lining made in step 3 in the middle of one length of one of the 42″ (54″) lengths of embroidered ribbon trim, wrong sides together, matching one middle pin to the other. Topstitch ¹/₈″ from the edge of each side (Fig. 4–4d). For strength, add a second row of stitches next to the first. Repeat for the second strap. Press and set straps aside.

Step 5. Pick up one of the two large 13″ x 15″ (21″ x 23″) pieces of canvas for front and back. Hold it so that the long 15″ (23″) sides are in right and left hands. Fold ¹/₂″ on the top of each 13″ (21″) end to the wrong side and press. Then fold again 1¹/₂″ (1″) and press. Center the top of the wallet pocket, ¹/₂″ depth, under one of the freshly folded tops, baste, and stitch across the full length of the folded edge in matching thread (Fig. 4–4e). Place a second row for added strength. Repeat for the other side, without the wallet pocket. If you have a seam guide on your machine, it's a good idea to use it on this top fold.

Step 6. To attach the strap, pin wallet pocket up and out of the way (Fig. 4–4f). Take the large outer piece with the pocket pinned up and place one of the prepared strap handles in an inverted U shape from point L to point R (Fig. 4–5). The outer edge of the

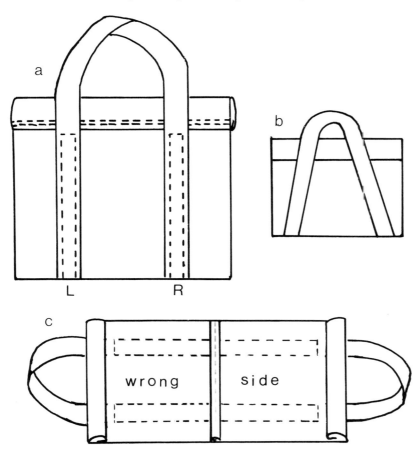

Fig. 4–5 Placement of straps a. Small bag: straps are placed in U shape, 2″ from edge. b. Large bag: straps are placed in an inverted V to support large bag 4″ from bottom and 6″ from top edge. c. Attaching the two halves together with a welt-type seam.

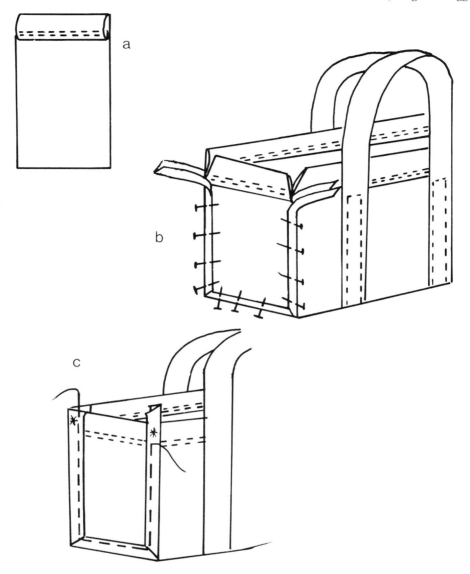

Fig. 4–6   Inserting side panels a. Making the side panel. b. Pinning binding to outside seam, starting binding 1″ above top fold. c. Start binding at point *. Top of binding is tucked to the inside of bag, point *, and hidden in fold of seam.

strap should measure 2″ from the side edges of the piece it is to be placed on (Fig. 4–5*a*); for the big bag, 6″ at top and 4″ at bottom (Fig. 4–5*b*). Begin the stitching at the bottom of the braid, ¹/₈″ from edge. Stitch up to the double row of stitching on top of canvas; stitch across the strap and back down on the other side of the braid. Repeat for the other end of the strap. Release pins on wallet pocket so that it hangs free. Repeat for the other half of the canvas bag.

Step 7. Place the right sides of the back and front together. Stitch across the bottom ¹/₂″ from the raw edge. Turn one raw edge of the seam allowance evenly over the other edge; then topstitch the seam allowance on the inside. This is called a flat felled seam (Fig. 4–5*c*).

Step 8. To make the sides, turn down one of the short ends of the side pieces ¹/₂″ and press. Turn again 1¹/₂″ (1″). Press and sew with a double row of stitches. Repeat for the second side (Fig. 4–6*a*).

Step 9. Pin one side section at a time onto the bag. There is ¹/₂″ seam allowance that is to *face the outside of the bag*. Begin pinning just below the fold at the top of each side. Continue pinning until the square is formed at the bottom. A small ¹/₄″ notch may be cut into the corner of the outer shell of the bag at the point where it rounds the side panel. Start to apply the double-faced braid 1″ above the top of the bag. Replace each pin with the double-fold braid (Fig. 4–6*b*). Fold the 1″ excess to the inside of the bag so that the raw edge of the braid is hidden in the seam on the inside (Fig. 4–6*c*). Baste the binding to the outer rim, squaring off the bottom corners. On the lower corners, the binding will stretch over the outer shell of the bag, but may need to be mitered at the inside corners.

Step 10. Stitch by machine with zipper foot and matching colored thread all the way round, pivoting at the two bottom corners. Because of the convenience of the double-fold braid, only one row of stitches is needed. Repeat for the other side section.

Step 11. This bag would hold its shape better with a floorboard: See instructions in Chapter Two.

DUFFLE BAG

This deluxe version of the classic multipurpose roll-style duffle is a wardrobe must. Designed to carry heavy loads without sagging, it features ring-around handles and an easy zip opening. The short, squat size is designed to be carried easily by women and the youthful traveler. The size as given will accommodate a sleeping bag as well: The handles can be left off and the bag can be tied to the backpack frame. The pattern can be scaled down to become a handbag, or enlarged to accommodate two or more sleeping bags for car or boat travel. The firmer the fabric the better for the shape of this bag. It has been styled here with contrasting color piped seams, but will look great with outside double-fold braid seams. See color Fig. 5, off-white bag with multicolor striped straps, and Fig. 4–1.

MATERIALS

> outside fabric for main body of bag: 1 yard of 45″ or 1¹/₂ yards of 30″, such as drill, canvas, denim, upholstery
> one heavy-duty 20″ separating zipper
> piping: 3 yards of premade upholstery piping
> 3 yards of canvas webbing luggage tapes: needs no backing. (*Option*—use braid tapes or self-straps, piecing if necessary)
> heavy-duty thread and #8 needle

PREPARATION

The duffle has a very easy pattern. Cut one rectangle 40″ x 22″, seam allowance included. Cut two round circles 12¹/₄″ in diameter, plus ¹/₄″ seam allowances.

ASSEMBLY

Step 1. Fold the large rectangle in half lengthwise, then in half crosswise and press lightly. These folds will be your guides for placement of straps.

Step 2. The strap is one continuous length, made 108″ long of luggage webbing. (Optional: The straps may be made from self material, using method two under strap instruction in Chapter Two. For a decorative strap using fancy woven braids or embroidery trims, completely back the braid trim with the outside fabric as shown in strap method one.) Using the intersecting cross of the lengthwise and crosswise folds, measure 4″ to either side of the lengthwise fold and place two pins on the crosswise fold. Starting at pin-point * (Fig. 4–7a), pin the strapping out to the raw edge and loop it around, leaving approximately 18″ above the raw edges at the center point. Bring it back down on the other side of the lengthwise fold, crossing the other pin marking. Loop it again on the opposite raw edge and bring back to point *. Fold the raw end of the strap back against its wrong side about 1/2″ or place the two raw edges together and zigzag over the union.

Measure from the center crosswise fold, 16″ on either side of each strap, and place four pins as markers. Begin stitching at the cross fold. Stitch up one side of the strap, cross over at pin marking, and go back down the other side. Cross over the strap at the second pin in marking and proceed to point *. Repeat this stitching for the other strap, using Fig. 4–7a as a guide.

Step 3. Fold and press the 3/4″ seam allowance to the wrong side at the two 22″ ends of the rectangle (under the newly made loop handles). Separate the zipper and center. Place the edge of the fold flush against the edge of the teeth of the zipper, baste, and sew

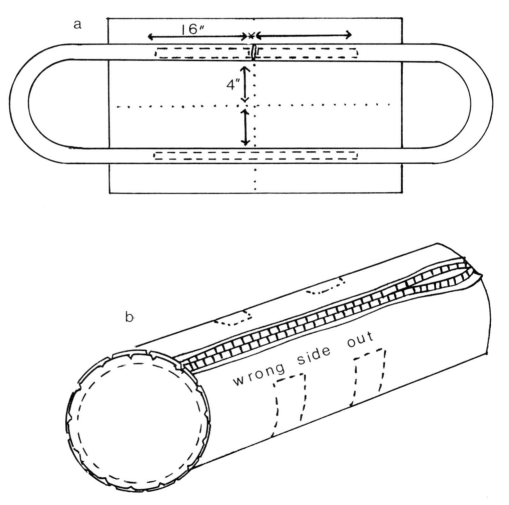

Fig. 4–7 Duffle bag a. Placing and sewing on straps. b. Putting the ends on duffle. Bag shown wrong-side out. Keep *zipper partially open* when working.

down permanently, using the zipper foot. Place a second row of stitches $^1/_8''$ to $^1/_4''$ from the first, being sure to catch the zipper tape underneath. Repeat for the other side and other half of the zipper.

Step 4. Close the zipper three-quarters of the way and proceed to place one of the round ends against one of the funnel-shaped ends of your main portion, right sides together (Fig. 4–7b). If you want the ends to remain noticeably round, then add decorative piping to the ends. It is attached first to the round end pieces, using the zipper foot (see instructions for piping in Chapter One). See color Fig. 5, beige duffle trimmed with navy piping. It may be necessary to notch the edge of the round end piece and slash along the edges of the main portion. Notch and slash only to a depth of $^1/_8''$, which is half the width of the $^1/_4''$ seam allowance. Stitch permanently with a double row of stitches, using zipper foot. Repeat for the other side. Open the zipper and turn right-side-out. Remember when packing the duffle to place the heaviest clothing in the center under the long straps and the lightest weight articles at the ends. This will prevent the bag from sagging.

Optional Zipper Treatment: If you cannot get a long separating zipper when making the bag longer, then get two half the size and place the ends at the outer edges of the bag and the tab pulls both at the center. The bag will zip open to the right and to the left.

Optional Monogram: Place at the point where the stitching stops on straps (or 16″ inches up from the center fold). Put monogram on before step 2, using the fold lines as a guide.

BACKPACK

The backpack is one of the best received of all gifts for the young at heart. It can be made rather small for the grade schooler or larger, with enough room for a good picnic lunch, for a chummy group. Because this hangs on the wearer's back it must be a rather stiff construction (see color Fig. 5 and Fig. 4–8). The pattern given is for a large size and sports outside seams covered with double-fold braid. To keep this closure adjustable to the contents inside, I have chosen to use the traditional loop and string.

There are two suggestions for fabric and one basic construction. The first group of fabrics would include canvas, real blue-jean denim, upholstery, real pillow ticking, or drill. This type of fabric can be handled easily without any additional support. The second group includes all other sportswear and drapery type fabrics that need the support of an interlining. This is where piecing together an attractive patchwork design of squares or rectangles from the scrap pile will be decorative and a challenge to the crafter. In this classification, fabrics such as prints can be used and quilted with novelty stitching right to an interlining fabric like drill. The drill will act as both interlining and regular lining. This backpack is worked in a patchwork pattern print that has been quilted to the drill fabric by machine. The batting is polyester. One word about the straps: They must be strong. If you are making self straps, use a strong, perhaps double, strip of belt interlining inside. Luggage webbing has a design on both sides and need not be lined or interlined. This is basically a heavy-duty bag and a heavy-duty #18 needle should be used, along with heavy-duty thread. Make sample stitches on your fabric; use the smallest number of stitches to the inch as possible.

MATERIALS

classification 1 fabric: $1^1/_2$ yards 45″ outer fabric
classification 2 fabric: $1^1/_2$ yards 45″ outer fabric; 2 yards 30″ interlining; 1 piece 15″ x 53″ batting

Fig. 4–8   Backpack of patchwork print, quilted to drill lining.

8 yards of double-faced braid
three 1″ to 1¹/₂″-diameter rings (metal preferred)
washable belt interfacing, 2″ x 80″, for lined straps
two buckles to make the back strap adjustable

PREPARATION

The back, front, and flap are all cut in one piece with two separate side insets; ¹/₂″ seam allowance is included (Fig. 4–9a). You will be able to see just how easy it is to vary the pattern. The finished size of the article will be 14″ high by 4″ deep, with two 40″ straps. Cut the flap and bottom ends of side insets with rounded corners. After cutting out the interlining, place markings lightly in pencil on the lining, using Fig. 4–9a as a guide.

ASSEMBLY

Step 1. If you have chosen a fabric from the second group, then place the batting between the wrong side of the outside fabric and the interlining and quilt, after cutting out.

Step 2. Cut two pieces of double-fold braid 4″ long. Stitch together edges of the open side, the folded side, and across both freshly cut ends to help prevent fraying. Fold each newly made tab in half over a ring. Place the ends of the two ring tabs against the raw edges of the *front* portion on the right side, as indicated on the pattern with *x* marks. Stitch into the ¹/₂″ seam allowance (Fig. 4–9b). Cut a third tab 6″ long. Prepare as above.

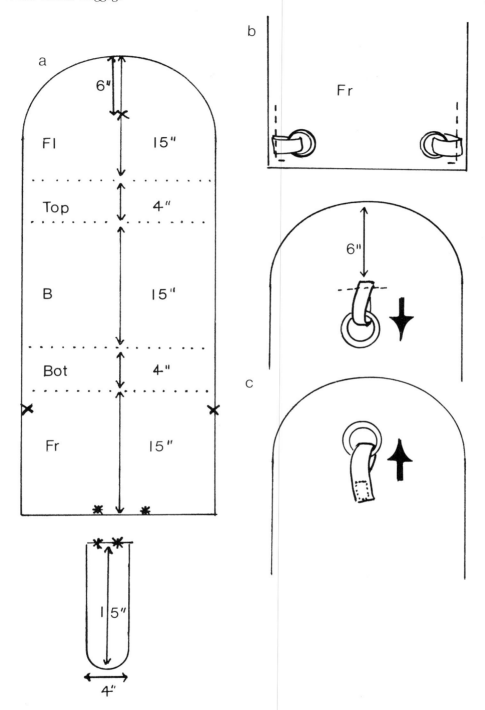

Fig. 4–9 Backpack assembly a. One-piece pattern for backpack will be 53″ long x 14″ wide and the two sides are 4″ x 15″. Indicate fold markings (dots) on wrong side of fabric. b. Placing the ring tabs on front. c. Placing the ring tab on flap.

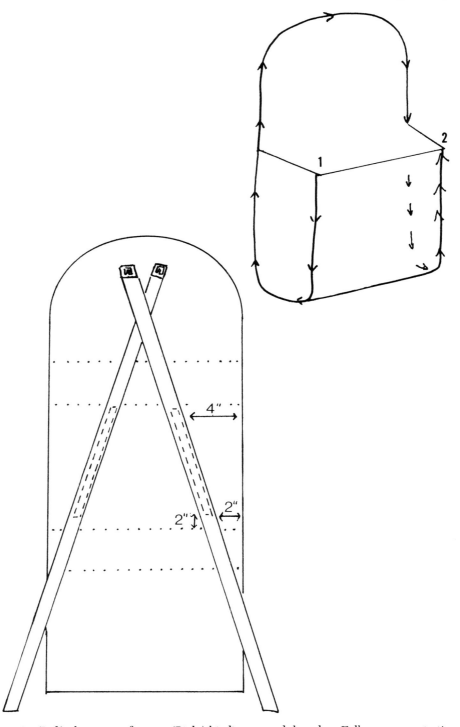

Fig. 4–10   (*Left*) placement of straps. (*Right*) binding around the edge. Follow arrows, starting at 1 and ending at 2. One side of bag is hidden, but binding passes down the back, around, and up the front.

Place the remaining tab at the *x* mark on the flap on right side of fabric. Place in position so that the ring is toward the top of the bag and the remaining ends are all at the *x* mark (Fig. 4–9c). Stitch across twice at *x*. Flip the ring and tab down toward edges of flap and secure with a double row of stitches (See Fig. 4–9c).

Step 3. To make straps, cut two lengths of fabric 4¹/₂″ wide by 41″ long. Line with washable belt interlining. Use strap method two given earlier (see Fig. 2–1). They should be 2″ wide by 40″ long for the medium-sized adult. Remember to tuck into wrong side on both ends and sew across. Center against the right side of the back portion in the form of an inverted V (Fig. 4–10). Stitch the two lengths of strap that touch the back piece; stitch across the top and bottom for additional support.

Step 4. Cover the top raw edges of the two side panels and the top portion of the front, indicated with double stars, in Fig. 4–9, with double-fold braid. Just slip it over the raw edges and topstitch.

Step 5. Fit the side panel into the U shape formed by the front, bottom, and back. Match the binding on the top of the front to that on the tops of the sides. Pin in place. Pin the raw edges of the main portion of the shell and sides to the outside, starting at point 1 in Fig. 4–10. Cover the two raw edges, the same as for the canvas open tote (Fig. 4–6), but rounding the bottom corners. Continue up and around the flap of the backpack and down on the other side to unite the second side, finishing up at point 2 (Fig. 4–10). Fold the 1″ excess at the top at points 1 and 2 to the inside of the bag so that the raw edge of the braid is hidden in the seam on the inside (see Fig. 4–6). Baste very carefully and then stitch permanently.

Step 6. Fold a 30″ length of double-fold braid in half. Place the folded end through the loop on the flap, about 2″. Then draw the two free-hanging ends through the loop, catching the ring as you pull the two free-hanging ends down. Separate the two free-hanging ends and place through the loops on the sides of the bag and bring to the center of the bag and tie to keep flap closed. To try on, fill pack with crushed newspapers or a pillow. Adjust strap and stitch buckle in place or stitch closed.

FLIGHT BAG

The flight bag is a good choice for any woman on the go—a spacious square box of fabric that neatly folds for easy storage on a shelf. The sturdy zipper, strong straps, and hidden floorboard give high-fashion fabrics all the support they need for years of wear at mini price. (See color Fig. 3, solid-color turquoise bag.) The fabrics that do the best job are canvas, denim, upholstery, heavyweight tapestry, or slipcover fabric. It would look smart in the new suede-finish fabric or some of the prequilted sport cottons supported with a backing of drill cloth.

The size can be adjusted from the travel sizes to the attache size. Handles can be made of self fabric, contrasting strip luggage webbing, or braid trims, and there are a variety of pockets that can be added, from the simple patch to the special zip-top personal pocket discussed earlier. There are many options offered for this bag, such as using plain seams sewn twice or piped seams. Zippers used throughout are the regular metal jacket zippers put out by all the big zipper companies supplying the home sewing market. A long upholstery zipper can be used, if available. A rigid floorboard allows it to carry heavy loads without sagging.

Cut the pattern pieces as given in Fig. 4–11a, ¹/₂″ seams included. Label all pieces on the wrong side, lightly in pencil. They may be trimmed down to suit your needs. Round the eight corners on pattern piece #1. Use a compass or plain water glass.

MATERIALS

	Outer Fabric	Heavy-Duty Separating Zipper	Washable Belt Interlining	Optional Piping
large size (22″ x 15″)	2 yards	two 20″	1″ x 86″	5 yards
small size (14″ x 10″)	1¹/₂ yards	two 11″	1″ x 54″	3 yards

¹/₄″ plywood or sturdy cardboard for optional floorboard

CUTTING INSTRUCTIONS

	Cut	Large	Small
#1—front and back (round off corners)	2	22″ x 15″	14″ x 10″
#2—top and sides	2	45″ x 4″	24¹/₂″ x 3″
#3—bottom and sides	1	48″ x 6¹/₂″	28″ x 4¹/₂″
#4—strap	2	42″ x 3″	28″ x 2¹/₂″
#5—inside floorboard	1	14″ x 6¹/₂″	10″ x 4¹/₂″

ASSEMBLY

Step 1. Make the handles, using the washable belt interfacing. Follow strap method two in Chapter Two, leaving the narrow ends raw. Place one strap against the front of the bag in an inverted U shape (Fig. 4–11*b*). After basting, stitch up from bottom to 2″ from the top on both sides of the strap. Stitchery makes interesting patterns and it is decorative to use contrasting thread and a novel pattern of stitches. The pattern may be lightly drawn for the machine to follow. Repeat for the second strap and the back of the bag.

Step 2. Placing the zipper in the top: Fold to the wrong side the 1″ seam allowance on one lengthwise side only of the two top-side pieces #2. Press. Center the two pull-tab ends of zippers at the center of the folded edges of two #2 pieces, leaving only about ¹/₂″ space between each zipper head (Fig. 4–11*c*). Fold the raw end tabs back to the inside. Place the zipper teeth next to the freshly made folded edge and stitch down with a double row of stitches. Make sure the second row of stitches is alongside the first. Only the zipper teeth will show. When finished, treat as one piece (Fig. 4–11*c*). The zippers will be shorter than the two #2 pieces. Finished, it will be 6¹/₂″ wide (the part of the zipper that shows will be about ¹/₂″).

Step 3. Fold the seam allowances of both short ends of #5 to the wrong side and stitch down. Center the wrong side of #5 against the wrong side of #3 and baste along the raw edges in the seam allowance (Fig. 4–12*a*).

Step 4. Stitch the narrow ends of band #2, with its zipper sewn in, to the narrow ends of #3, right sides together. You will notice that this is larger than the circumference of the two #1 pieces. The adjustment is made by turning upward the lower band #3 and lapping it over the ends of the zippered band #2. Baste across the fold on both sides. This will then be the proper fit of the circular band around the front and back pieces. The reason no absolute measurement can be given for the fold is simply that the various fabrics used will vary a bit in sewing.

Optional Piping: On both front and back pieces #1, sew piping to the right side of both pieces with the seam allowance of the piping lying within the seam allowance of the

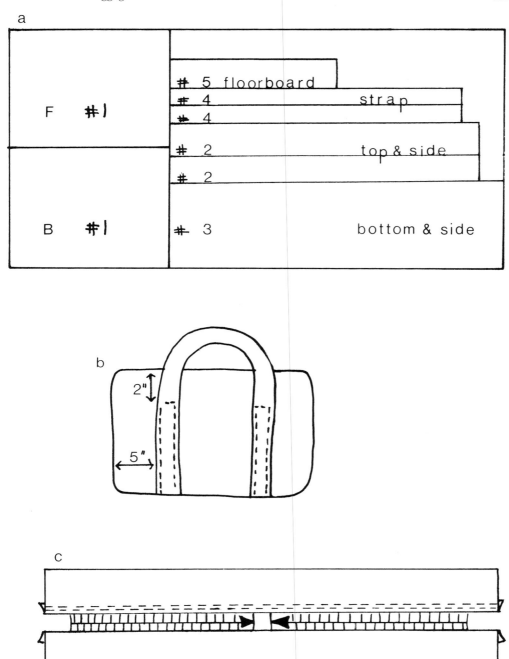

Fig. 4–11 Flight bag layout and assembly a. Approximate layout of flight bag for canvas fabric width. b. Placing strap onto front and back pieces. c. Placing the zippers into top and side pieces. Note double row of stitching on one side. It is suggested for both sides.

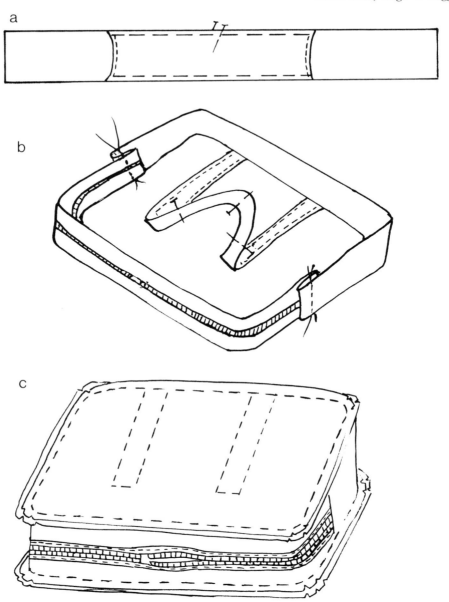

Fig. 4–12   Finishing the flight bag a. Setting the band to hold floorboard in place. b. Fitting band around the front. Fold up additional material in sides. c. Leave zipper open before fitting final bottom side onto the circling band.

#1 pieces. Clip the seam allowance in three places at the corners before turning. Start and finish at the bottom of the bag.

Step 5. Pin the handle part of the straps back against its #1 piece with safety pins. Baste the piece selected as the front to the newly made circumference band, right sides together. A $1/2''$ seam allowance has been suggested, but you can work with less if you like (Fig. 4–12*b*). Use your zipper foot and position it to the right as it faces you. Sew permanently through all the layers—the band, the front, and the floorboard band (and the optional piping). Stitch a second row $1/8''$ from the first set of stitches for added strength.

Optional: For a fine finish for handbag size, fold bias tape over the raw edge to the other side, but not beyond the freshly sewn double row of stitches. Trim the seam allowance, if necessary, to have the tape cover all the raw edges. Baste the tape in place and then stitch permanently just within the first rows of stitches. As another option, use the zigzag stitch on the machine over the raw seam edges if you like. If making the smaller size for a handbag, it is most important to cover the seams due to the hard wear the bag will receive.

Step 6. Open the zipper about 3″ and repeat step 5 for placing the back onto the bag (Fig. 4–12c).

Step 7. The bag is inside-out before you. Slip a floorboard approximately 5″ x 21$\frac{1}{2}$″ into the bottom of the bag, along the open funnel made in step 3. Floorboard can be made of very sturdy cardboard or of $\frac{1}{4}$″ plywood, with the corners rounded so they do not wear a hole in the bag. This is an optional feature and may be eliminated if the bag is to be used only on car trips or for short overnights.

Step 8. Slip your fingers into the opening in the zipper teeth as suggested in step 5 and open the rest of the zipper. Turn the bag right-side-out. On the right side, place a tri-

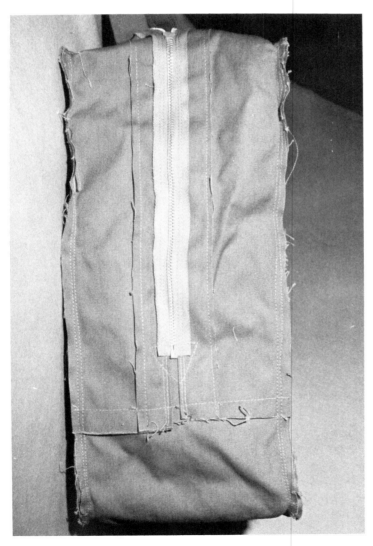

Fig. 4–13   Inside of bag: Note reinforcing stitches at zipper base.

angle or square of stitches on the side where the foldovers occur (Fig. 4–13). Open both zippers seven-eighths of the way and place in machine. Stitch through the fabric on the outside, crossing the bottom of the zipper very carefully. You may have to skip a stitch if needle will not penetrate through the center of the teeth—just continue on. Now you're ready to pack and go—Happy Landing!

SPACEMATE SINGLE SUITER AND DRESS-LENGTH FOLDOVER BAG

The neatest way to pack clothing for carry-on convenience is to hang it in a space-mate bag. These styles are planned as travelers, but can be made with equal success as closet accessories. First, the short, single-suit size. Second, the longer dress size with triple handles (see color Fig. 3, yellow and turquoise for suit bag and turquoise trimmed in white for dress bag). The dress bag can hang full length if there is room, or fold gently on its triple set of handles. Both are truly the ultimate in long-trip comfort.

The fabric used should be lightweight canvas, denim, sportswear duck or poplin, ticking, or drapery. The fabrics may be backed with plastic sheeting to make them dustproof and waterproof. Most canvas is already waterproof, but sometimes you can find other waterproof fabrics if you ask for them. Check on dirt-resistant finishes, too. Seer-sucker is one example of a really sharp-looking, lightweight fabric that needs to be backed with another fabric to give it body.

These spacemate bags are the lightest weight of all the bags, but their strength and long life will be enhanced with *metal zippers*. They are further embellished with outside seams covered with double-fold braid, a super easy construction. The seam techniques are explained in detail in Chapter One. The outsides may be enlivened with zip-top pockets. Plan the pockets before other construction starts. Monogramming and appliques can be added, but should be added before assembly and located near the top of the bag. A quick technique for the monogramming-applique idea is to use iron-on patches which are generally used for the repair of jeans and play clothing. Just cut the design out and apply with a hot iron.

To shape the basic pattern: Using a standard 18″ hanger that you plan to use in your spacemate bag, trace the shape onto large brown wrapping paper. Add 1″ to widen the shape to approximately 20″, add ½″ seam allowance, and then decide on the overall length of the bag. The single suiter should be about 36″ to 39″ long, the three-hanger dress bag about 48″ long (for evening gown, 60″), but this length is adjustable. It stands to reason that a tall person will have longer clothing than a short one. The shoulders create a rounded look at the top of the pattern and the bottom of the bag should be square, with rounded corners for ease in applying the binding. They are made with outside seams covered with double-fold braid. The dress bag will have 4″-wide side insets. To make the inset, measure the circumference of the pattern you have, then cut a piece of fabric that length by 4″ wide. Piece it if necessary in an inconspicuous spot.

MATERIALS

	Fabric	Double-Fold Braid	Separating Zipper	Washable Belt Interlining
Single Suiter	2½ yards, 36″ or 45″	6½ yards	one 22″ and one 14″ or one 36″	—
Dress Bag (48″ long)	3⅔ yards, 36″ or 45″	9 yards	two 22″	1½ yards, 1″ wide

Single-Suit Bag

Using the pattern you have, cut one piece of fabric for the front of the bag and a second piece for the back, *1" wider but not longer.* Fold the second piece in half lengthwise and cut it down the middle, making it two pieces. Fold and press each freshly cut center $1/2"$ to the wrong side, forming a seam allowance. Place on either side of the metal zipper teeth with the 22" zipper being placed upside-down in the upper portion of the opening, meeting the shorter zipper placed upright in the lower half (Fig. 4–14a). Sew the zipper down permanently, stitching close to the edge. This side of the bag should be the same width as the first piece cut. Trim the top of the rounded hanger opening so it is about 2" in diameter at the most. Place the two pieces together with *wrong sides* touching. If the back is a little bit big, trim it down. Pin the outer raw edges all the way around.

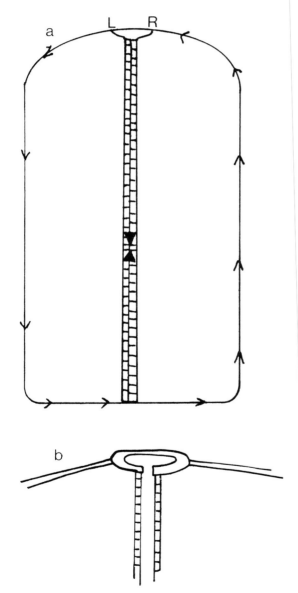

Fig. 4–14   Assembling spacemate a. Placing two zippers into bag. b. Placing binding around hanger opening of bag.

Starting at point L in Fig. 4–14*a*, place the double-fold braid over both raw edges and proceed down the side, around the bottom, catching end of zipper in the braid, and up the other side to point R. With a separate piece of braid, center and circle the hanger opening, covering all raw edges of the braid trim (Fig. 4–14*b*). Tuck the raw ends of the braid back against itself for finishing and stitch with the machine. For a woman's bag, 24″ lengths of braid may continue down the front and be tied in a bow for decoration (see color Fig. 3).

Dress-Length Foldover Bag

Using the pattern you have, adjust it for the length of approximately 48″ and a width of 22″. Cut one piece of fabric for the front of the bag and a second piece for the back of the bag, 1″ wider but not longer. This bag will require an inset band all the way round to allow for three hangers Measure the circumference of the pattern, add an inch on either end, and cut a piece that length, or piece it to equal that length, 142″ for pattern suggested. It should be 5″ wide, including ½″ seam allowance. Measure for the length of the

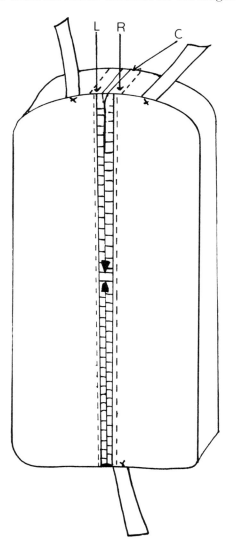

Fig. 4–15   Placing the side inset band onto the back with three straps caught under binding. Note: Bottom strap is just off zipper tapes.

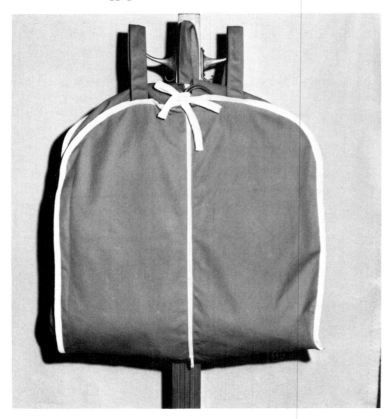

Fig. 4–16 The folded
bag can be carried by
slipping the three loops
over arm, or by the
hangers.

zipper from the hanger opening down to almost the bottom of the bag. If you cannot get
one zipper that long, then use two separating zippers, each 22″ long. Place one at the bottom with its pull-tab at the middle of the bag, and the other with its pull-tab meeting the
lower one and its tail end at the top hanger opening. The bag will open from the middle,
one zipper going down and one going up.

ASSEMBLY

Step 1. Cut three short self-carrying straps, 14″ x 3″. Prepare straps, using strap
method two, supporting straps with 1″ washable belt interlining, leaving the ends with
raw edges. Set straps aside.

Step 2. Fold the larger back piece in half lengthwise and cut it down the middle,
making it two pieces. Fold each freshly cut center ¹/₂″ to the back, forming a seam allowance on each side. Place the folded edge on either side of the metal zipper teeth, with
one zipper having its tab in the middle of the bag and its tail at the bottom, and the second zipper having its tab in the middle and its tail 1″ from the top. Sew the zippers down
permanently, stitching close to the edge (Fig. 4–15). This side of the bag should be the
same width as the first piece cut. With this large piece before you, measure out 4″ on either side of the zipper opening and mark an *x*, as shown. Place the second piece on top
and repeat, matching the markings on the front. On the second piece, place an *x* mark 1″
to the right of zipper at the center bottom. These are indications for the three strap place-
ments.

Step 3. Placing the long side insets into the bag: At both 5″ ends of the long side inset
band, turn the seam allowance back 1″. Working on the outside with wrong sides

together, pin one long edge of the side inset band against the piece planned for the back (with the zippers). Start pinning at point L and continue all the way around the bag until you come back to the hanger opening at point R. Remember now that this is to have both raw edges facing outward (Fig. 4–15). Pin one end of the three straps to the x marks, matching raw edges, so that the straps lay back against the band portions. Starting at point L again, baste the double-fold braid over the two raw edges and, where necessary, over band ends. Continue basting all the way around and finish at point R. Turn the raw ends of the braid back against itself and stitch permanently, being careful to get close to the edges of the braid. Check often to make sure that you are catching both edges of the braid in one row of permanent stitches.

Step 4. Pin the front of the bag to the other side of the band, pinning the straps to the second set of x marks on the bag front. Pin the braid on top, starting at point C, and continue around the bag, covering the other raw ends of the straps as you proceed. Finish by folding back the end of the braid tape and covering the starting point.

The bag can be hung using the two upper straps, or it can be folded in half for carrying, slipping the three straps over one forearm, the strap at the bottom slipping in the middle between the two at the top, as shown in Fig. 4–16.

5

Hats

The hat is the indispensable fashion item for today. It is worn as a fashion accessory with the versatile sportswear that dominates today's wardrobe. The most important look is the fabric hat. Using materials readily available to the home sewer, it is soft, comfortable, so easy to make, and may be made of washable fabric. The few materials that have to be dry cleaned will not have to be blocked by a hatter.

The hats offered here are of differing styles to carry you from daytime to evening. More important, they are of differing construction techniques. By learning the various techniques, the crafter can apply the basic ideas to create new and more novel hats as they come into fashion.

Let's begin with the hatter's vocabulary.

The *crown* is the part that covers the upper part of the scull; its boundaries would be the hairline above the forehead and the portion of hair above the ears.

The *brim* is the part of the hat that extends beyond the crown of the hat and generally stretches out or is folded back against the crown in some manner. Some hats are brimless and just hug the crown.

The *peak* is used occasionally as a firm appendage attached to the front of the crown in order to shade the eyes. Soft, woven fabric hats generally do have linings and almost always have a band around the inside of the crown to cover the raw seams and create a smooth fit. Knit hats have an easier construction, due to the fact that the fabric will not ravel.

There are two main styles given here. The easiest to make are the soft styles, like the beret, the auto cap, the turban, and the knit mini-madcaps. They are enhanced by the softness of the fabric. This type of hat can be worn many ways and is meant to complement the shape of the face. The second type includes shaped classics, like the cloche that depends on the firmness of the fabrics and its interfacings to give it definition. The novelty of the trainman's cap depends on the crown standing away from the head and the rather large peak. The fake fur fabrics are so firm that they almost stand up by themselves, as in the toque style.

COPYING AND MAKING PATTERNS

Most patterns given here are rectangles, which are very easy to cut from a piece of fabric, with or without a premade pattern. When working with knits, it is most important

123

to note the *direction of the stretch.* As an added precaution before cutting, test the stretch in the knit and baste a large running stitch in a contrasting color in the direction of the stretch. Patterns indicate stretch with triple arrows at the end of a straight line.

The actual-size patterns are given shaded, including the 1/4″ seam allowance. The best way to use it is to place a piece of paper, such as typing paper, over the shaded area, copy the pattern and transfer to cardboard (or Bristol board or oak tag found in the art supply store).

Some patterns call for making round circles. The quickest way is to tie a rather thin string to a pencil. At the other end, tie the string to a large pin, such as hat or upholstery pin. The length between the pinpoint and the pencil point will be *one-half the diameter* of the circle. Place the pin in the center of the fabric, on the wrong side, and draw a full circle. Be sure to hold the string taut when making the circle (Fig. 5–1).

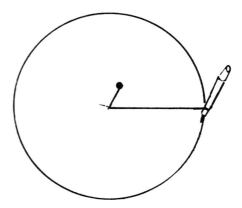

Fig. 5–1 Making a circle the quick, old-fashioned way. Remember that the line (radius) is half the diameter of the circle.

FIGURING YARDAGE

Yardage requirements are figured in the simplest of all manners. For each hat, the fabric requirement is given in minimum squared-off inches. The reason is that this is a creative craft article and it is the author's fervent hope that the reader will be experimenting with many fabrics. Fabrics suggested here come in many widths—fake furs and felt at 60″ wide; drapery fabrics, dress flannels, and many knits 54″ wide; lace, hand-printed silks, and velvets often come only 36″ wide. Other sources for hat materials are the remnant table and one's leftover scrap bag. When purchasing fabric, come to the nearest yard that the dealer will sell.

MEASURING AND FITTING

Measuring. Taking the measurements for your own hat, you will probably find that you have come close to the standard American head size of 22″. If you have ever gone to the shops to try on hats, only to find that they are a bit floppy, then you may have a smaller head size; or if you have found that the hats sit on top and never really come down far enough, you may have a larger head size.

All the hats here are figured on a 22″ standard woman's head; you may need to make your hat a little bit smaller or larger. You will need to measure the circumference of your head at a place where the hat will be worn. Use Fig. 5–2 as a guide for placement of a *high-crown* hat, such as the trainman's hat or English auto cap, or the *full-crown* for the cloche, or the *side-crown,* such as the classic French beret. The hats for men are given

Fig. 5–2   Measuring for a hat a. High-crown hat. b. Full-crown hat. c. Side-crown hat.

just a bit larger. The trainman's hat is also scaled down to fit boys, too. If you want to make the hat a bit bigger, then add the additional measurement to the crown pieces. Add this same measurement to either end of the brim pieces, also. It is best to plan all the seams at ¹/₄″ in hat crafting. If you cannot handle ¹/₄″ seams, then make ¹/₂″ seams and trim down after permanent stitching.

Fitting: As for fitting the hat at the crown, the entire crown must be made and pressed, then tried on before attaching the brim or peak. If the hat is to have a brim, then stick a thumb under the crown, which will allow for the additional bulk of the brim. If it is a brimless styling, then just add the width of the pinkie finger for the additional bulk to be added by the lining band, or stretch of the knit. Hats can easily be adjusted before the linings and brims are added. Any adjustments made in the outer fabric will have to be made to the lining. Some adjustments may be necessary due to the bulk of the fabric. For example, putting the brim on a velvet cloche is not the same as making the same hat in pique. The thickness of the fabric alone suggests adjustments.

Let us think about stretch fabrics that would be good for such hats as the turban and knit mini-madcaps. Stretch the knit against a ruler to see just how much stretch it really does have, but never stretch the knit when cutting. Remember to check the instructions to see which way the pattern runs and to make sure you have the stretch going the right direction around your head. The knit hat patterns will be marked with a triple set of arrows on each end of a straight line. It is sometimes confusing to remember the direction of the stretch, so loosely baste in a line of stitches to indicate stretch direction before cutting.

FABRICS

Fabric selection is dictated by what is available in the fabric fashion market. Fabrics come and go on the fashion scene, but hat shapes generally stay the same. It makes no difference if a fabric is knitted or woven. In fact, it is the wonderful knits available today that helped put so much punch back into hat wearing. What is important is the firmness or softness of the fabrics and the crafter's understanding of whether you are making a soft hat or one that requires a firm fabric to enhance the basic shape. When making hats that are soft, keep in mind that the linings, when called for, must be soft but opaque. When creating a hat that calls for the additional stiffness of an interlining, place the outside fabric over the interlining to make sure the interlining is firm enough to do the job. In hat crafting it makes no difference if the interlining is woven or nonwoven, such as Interlon by Stacy, Inc., or Pellon by Pellon Corp. To help with the selection of the fabric, follow the suggested outlines here.

Firm Styles: gabardine, chintz, homespun, organdy, bedford cord, pique, linen, felt, velveteen, sailcloth, corduroy, seersucker, denim, twill, duck, bengaline, double knits, fake furs, some drapery fabrics, quilted fabrics.

Soft styles: crepes, flannel, broadcloth, shantung, surah, satin, sateen, gingham, muslin, percale, pongee, velvet (panne or crushed), madras, poplin, kettle cloth, challis, honan, peau de soie, china silk, taffeta, chiffon, brocade, metallic lamé, lace and jersey knits, arnel/nylon knits, and sweater knits.

Brims and Peaks: To make the brim or peak of the hat really effective, you must first select the silhouette that you are trying to achieve. If you are making the brim on the cloche with knit material, then you will get a soft, floppy look. The same hat done in a velveteen or pique would need a firm, rather stiff brim to frame the face. To stiffen the brim, take the fabric selected for the outside and try it over several different interlinings. If the fabric is already stiff, then only a thin interlining will be needed; but if the fabric needs more body, then select a rather stiff interlining or use a double layer. If the fabric is bulky, such as velveteen, trim all excess interlining from the seam allowance after sewing. After the brim has been made, additional rows of stitching in concentric lines will give a firming effect.

The peak must be very stiff, whether it is large or small. Many layers of the interlining material may have to be used. The addition of concentric lines of stitching is a good idea to help make the peak firm. An alternate material for interlining the peak is a material called Permette by Conso Products Co., suggested for use in the envelope bag. Cut it *without* the seam allowance. Stitch together the outer fabric, top and bottom of the peak, turn to right side, and press. Slip the Permette between the wrong sides and run one row of topstitching around the outer edge of the peak to hold the Permette in its proper place.

Working with Knits: Knits are a special joy for hat crafters. Some readers may never have had the opportunity to work with knits. Polycore or all-polyester thread is a must. Cotton thread will not stretch with the knit fabric. Use a sharp needle and, if you see that it is snagging the yarn of the fabric, then a ball-point needle is needed. The newer machines have special stitches for knits and it would be wise to check the instructional material provided for this purpose. Make a few samples with the knit you are planning to use. One of the nicest things about knits is that their raw edges do not ravel.

DECORATIONS

Additional decorations, such as pins, buckles, feathers, frogs, beautiful flowers, and bias-cut sashes, can be added to hats (Fig. 5–3). These things can be purchased at trimming supply stores.

Making Bows

Bows are fun to make from ribbon or fabric. If ribbon is not available, make a fabric tube with the seam on the inside. Do not tie as is customary in bow making, but rather

Fig. 5–3   Hat decorations: Bows of striped and velvet ribbon—both on bias-cut sashing—flower, and tassel.

Fig. 5-4 Steps in making a tailored bow for hat and felt fabric flower.

make a tailored bow, using Fig. 5–4*a* as a guide. Cut a small 1″ end off the ribbon and set aside. Fold the large remaining portion of ribbon in half, right sides together, and stitch across the width of the ribbon about ³/₅″ from the fold. Open up and place the center fold against the stitching in center, then lightly press. Place one or two rows of small gathering stitches in the center of bow. Pull gathers gently and secure thread. Circle the smaller strip around the center, making sure no raw edges of top are showing. Secure in the back with a few stitches. For a very flat, tailored bow do not gather, but merely put the ribbon around center.

Making Felt Flowers

To make a felt flower, follow Fig. 5–4*b*. Cut three pieces of felt with assorted-size petals. Place the smaller ones on top of the larger ones. Place a few gathering stitches near the center and draw together gently—just enough to give the edges a little ripple or lift. The center can have one ball from a trimming called ball fringe. The center is made of two small flower centers found in trimming supply stores. These come on a long stem and have to have the stem pushed through a small slash in the center of all three pieces of felt, then the stem is secured on the back.

Special Effects

Many times you can purchase interesting scarves in shapes that will fit around the hats. Some can be folded on the diagonal and tied around the crown for a gossamer effect. The ends can be tucked in or allowed to hang loose. To use fabric, cut a strip on the bias and crush or tuck around the hat crown.

Appliques and embroidery can be added when the hat is finished, or before linings are in place.

Ribbons have long been a favorite decoration of the hat maker, to tie on or to attach. Washable satin and velvet are now available, along with the old washable standby, grosgrain. Plaid ribbons are available and, if formed into a sort of cockade with a self-covered button for the center, give a smashing look on a turned-back brim or a beret.

Making a friendship hat is fun. Make a hat and have all your friends embroider their names into your hat with some sort of fancy embroidered signature, such as a pierced heart, a little daisy, or a funny face.

COWL SNUGGLER

This easy to carry along styling fills big fashion needs. In the winter, in stretchy knits, this hat keeps you warm. At the beach, in stretch terrycloth, it covers up wet tresses smartly. For evening, in magical gossamer sheers, it adds a touch of illusion to any outfit (Fig. 5–5).

MATERIALS

One piece of knit fabric, at least 26″ by 20″. To measure for this hat, measure under the chin and just behind the hairline at the forehead—about 24″ to 25″. Add seam allowance on both sides. Cut a piece of knit fabric with the greatest stretch running the width of the above measurement. This will be the part that will go around the face. Cut its depth 20″ (Fig. 5–6*a*).

ASSEMBLY

Step 1. With right sides together, fold the fabric in half along the 20″ depth and stitch permanently. Press seam open.

Fig. 5–5   Cowl snuggler, made of polyester knit.

Step 2. Fold the ends of the tube 2″ to the wrong side (Fig. 5–6b). Raw ends of the knit fabric will not ravel and need not have edge folded again. Tack every 2″ around the tube, as shown. Tacking means that the thread must be broken when finished and started anew for each tack.

Step 3. Turn right-side-out and slip over the head. The lower end of the tube will cover the neck and the upper end will be around the face. Keep the seam under the chin.

VARIATIONS

Some machines today have stretch knit stitches. These could be used in place of the tacking. This hat could be made from woven fabric if the rectangle were cut on the bias, but this requires a careful measurement of the pattern against the selected width of fabric. If you work with sheers, use a small French seam.

Measurements given here apply to medium-size head. Enlarge, or decrease for children, by measuring from the top of the head to underneath chin. This type of cowl can be attached to the jewel neck of dress or blouse. It can be worn up as a hat or down around the neck as a cowl collar.

OPEN-CROWN HATS

The fabric should be crisp and firm, the color flattering to the hair, and, if a print is used, it should be very small, or all-over type. Eyelets and laces must be backed.

Open crowns are fair-weather complements. They are easy to make and require minimum yardage. They are always well received as gifts at boutique sales because they require minimum fitting. Both patterns can be scaled down to fit the young set. The

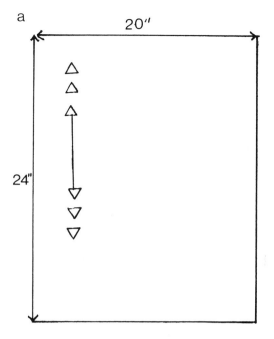

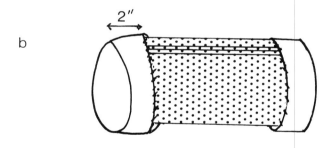

Fig. 5–6   Cowl snuggler a. Pattern for knit fabric. b. Turning edges back for tacking.

peaked sports hat can be made for men, using a very tailored fabric such as duck or cotton twill weaves. The second hat, the sunbrimmer, can be trimmed in a variety of ways: it can be tailored, or eyelet trimmed with flowers across the bands. See color Fig. 10; green calico with eyelet trim used for the open-crown peak and chintz with all-over floral print for the brim. Both have coordinated bags.

PEAKED SPORTS HAT

MATERIALS

    outer fabric: ³/₄ yard of 45″
    interlining for peak: 12″ x 20″ minimum (two layers of drill or one Permette preferred)
    elastic: ¹/₄″ by 4″

PREPARATION

    Cut one band of outside fabric on the bias, 4″ wide by 24″ long, seam allowance included. Press the raw edges ¹/₄″ to the wrong side and press in half lightly, wrong sides together. Make folded edges match. From the outside fabric, cut an upper and lower peak, using pattern given in Fig. 5–8. Cut two interlinings, or one interlining such as Permette, for the peak, *without seam allowance.*

ASSEMBLY

Step 1. Place the right sides of the outside fabric for the peak together (Fig. 5–7*a*). If trim is planned, such as eyelet, then place the raw edge of the trim in the larger curve in

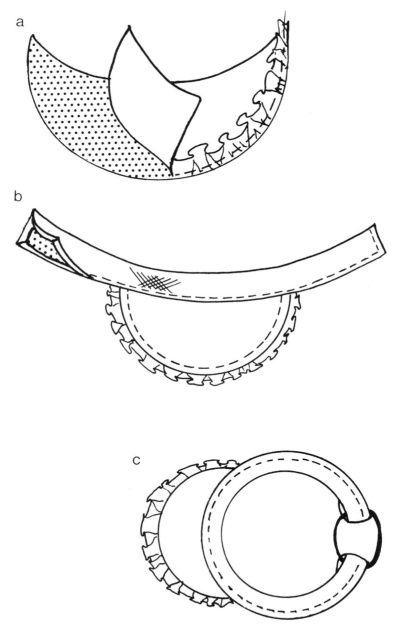

Fig. 5–7 Peaked sports hat a. Placing the peak and its lining together, with optional eyelet trim at edge. b. Setting finished peak into bias-cut band. c. Finish by threading elastic through two end tunnels of band.

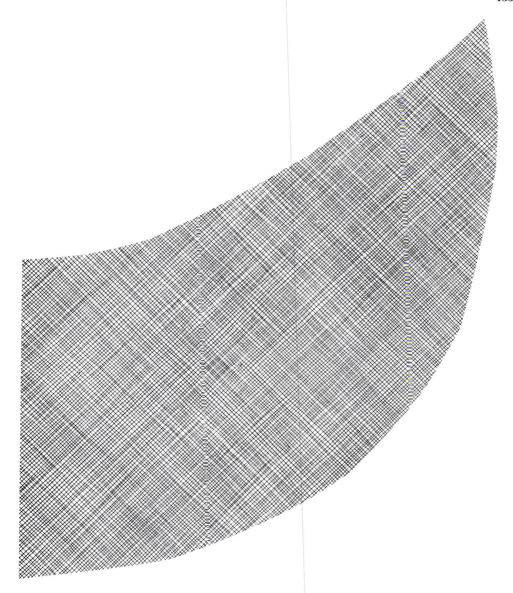

Fig. 5–8   Half-pattern for ladies' peaked hat.

the seam allowance. Stitch around the outside seam allowance, notch allowance, and turn to the right side. Press. Slip interfacing between wrong sides. Add additional stitchery, if necessary, to stiffen and decorate. Press and set aside.

Step 2. Find the center of the band and the center of the peak. Center the peak between the folded edges of the band as the pieces lay on the work surface before you. Baste in place as indicated in Fig. 5–7b. Stitch band closed $\frac{1}{8}''$ from the edge on the ends and across the band, catching the peak and its interlining in the seam. In the peak area, the band will have to conform to the concave line of the inner brim.

Step 3. Fit the hat around the head and fold the ends of the bands back against the wrong side. Stitch down two folds at each end to form tunnels. Place a circle of elastic through the two folds and adjust again to fit comfortably (Fig. 5–7c).

Since this hat is worn in warm weather, the elastic will wear out from the sun's heat, perspiration, and washing, but it can easily be replaced. An alternate would be to lap one end over the other at the back and fasten with Velcro snap dots, or make the band longer and tie the ends.

OPEN-CROWN SUNBRIMMER

This floppy but firm brim shades the face from the sun, but allows the head to remain cool by using a set of cross bands in top of the crown (Fig. 5–9). This hat can go to the beach, to the city, or to a wedding. Multi lines of stitching in brim create firmness.

Fig. 5–9   Open-crown sunbrimmer of printed chintz.

See color Fig. 10, printed drapery chintz. The only prerequisite for the hat is that the fabric remain rather stiff. See its matching bag which also turns into a sunning mat.

MATERIALS

outside fabric: 20″ long by 45″ wide
interfacing: 20″ long by 20″ wide

PREPARATION

Use pattern given for brimmer in Fig. 5–10*a*. Each brim pattern uses only 20″ x 20″. This hat could be made reversible, using scrap yardage. Cut two outside fabric, one interlining from pattern, and two bands, 3″ x 13″ long.

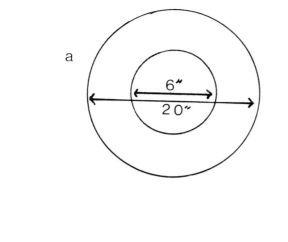

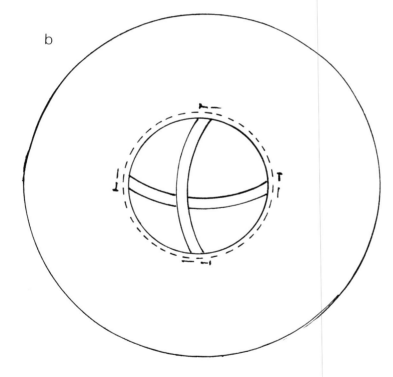

Fig. 5–10   a. Pattern for brimmer: outside diameter 20″, inside diameter 6″. b. Place bands within the inner circle of the brim and mark with pins for depth after trying on.

ASSEMBLY

Step 1. Fold each band over, using method two suggested in handbag straps. Do not use interlining unless fabric is very soft.

Step 2. Place the two outside circles against each other, right sides together. Place the interlining on top of one of the wrong sides, creating a triple layer. Pin and baste carefully and sew a seam around the outside of the triple-layer unit, $1/4''$ from the edge. Notch into seam allowances every inch. Turn to the right side and press. Using the outer edge, place several lines of stitching in a circle around the hat, either using concentric lines or varying the line widths. Stop stitching 1″ from inside circle of brim. Work from outer edge toward inside.

Step 3. Try on the brim. If it sits too high on your head, cut out ¹/₈″ at a time from the center circle opening until it fits comfortably. Open up the two outside pieces of the circle of the inner brim, exposing the interfacing. Trim ¹/₄″ off the interfacing and notch ¹/₈″ deep all the way around the two fabrics that form the inner circle. Turn each outside fabric back against itself and baste each separately.

Step 4. Place the two bands at right angles to each other and tack in center by hand. Position the two bands across the hat and slip the ends into the openings between the two brim pieces. Adjust so the hat fits comfortably, marking the depth with a pin (Fig. 5–10*b*). Withdraw the bands from the brim and trim to ¹/₄″ below pin marking. Replace into brim and baste the upper and lining portions of the brim together, catching the band ends in place. Sew permanently, ¹/₈″ from the edge. See matching beachmat pattern in Chapter Two.

TRAINMAN'S CAP

This cap is a jaunty addition to the casual wardrobe for train buffs and the young at heart. The kids like to wear them to school. They can be made in a blue and white striped denim, or a light or dark solid blue denim, and have no lining (see color Fig. 7).

Suggested sizes: A junior size would be for a head size 20″ to 21″; the larger head size for men and women would run from 22¹/₂″ to 24″ head circumference. The pattern is very adjustable and super easy to make.

MATERIALS

    junior and larger sizes: ¹/₂ yard of 30″ to 40″ wide fabric
    peak stiffening: 20″ x 20″ of drill or 10″ x 10″ of Permette (preferred)

Fig. 5–11   Trainman's caps, one of solid-color denim and one of striped ticking.

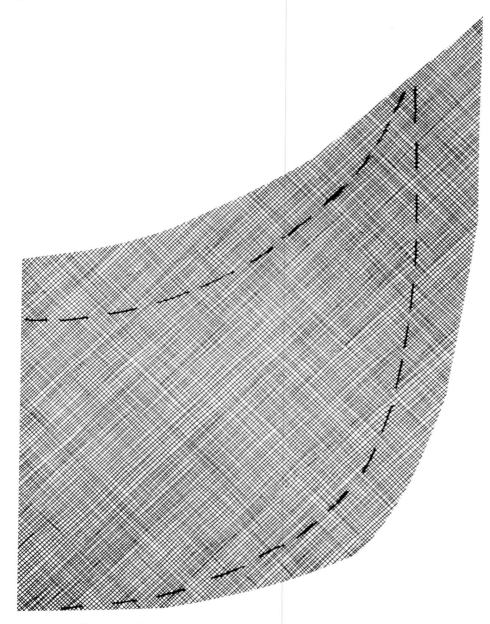

Fig. 5–12   Half-pattern of peak for adults. Broken line indicates junior size. Add seam allowance.

PREPARATION

A few points should be observed to make an authentic-looking trainman's cap. The stripes on the crown and the peak should run from front to back, not sidewise across the hat. It is also preferable to run the stripes on the band across the narrow width (Fig. 5–11). The first step is to measure the circumference of the head just above the ears, adding 1/2″ seam allowance to each end to determine the length of the band. Cut two bands, 1¹/₂″ wide each, by above measurement of head circumference. There are two peak patterns given in Fig. 5–12, one for adults and one for junior size. Add seam allowance. Cut two pieces of outside fabric, with seam allowance, and two very firm interlinings or one Permette interlining, without seam allowance. The crown is a complete circle. For a man's hat, cut the circle with a diameter of 16"; for a very large man, increase to 18". For the junior size, cut the circle with a diameter of 14½", seam allowance included. Check back to Fig. 5–1 for making circles quickly.

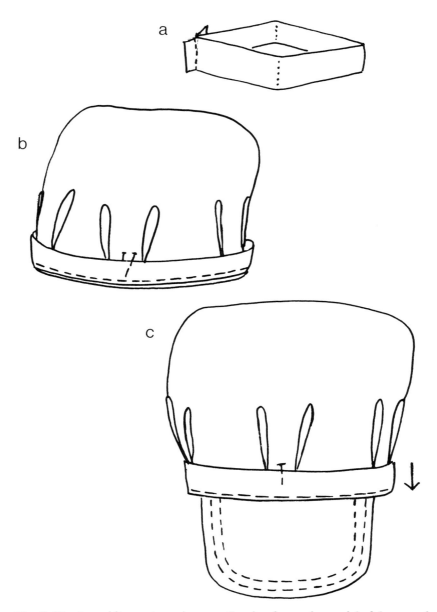

Fig. 5–13 Assembling trainman's cap a. Sew bands together and find four equal parts around each band. Mark with creases. b. Placing circle into one band, folded upward, right sides together. c. Fold two bands downward, away from crown. Turn the raw edge of each ¼" to wrong side. Peak seam allowance is tucked under the two edges and basted into place.

ASSEMBLY

Step 1. Make the peak as suggested in step 1, open-crown peaked sports hat. Press and set aside.

Step 2. Stitch the narrow ends of both bands together by placing the right sides together. Press seams open.

Step 3. Fold circular band in half to find the center. Crease. Fold again to find the equal sides (Fig. 5–13*a*). Fold the crown in half along the stripes (if stripes are used). Fold in half the opposite way to create four equal parts. Place the crown into the circle of one of the bands loosely, right sides together, matching up the four creases in the band to the four creases in the hat crown. The circumference of the crown will be larger than the circumference of the band. Take two tucks, toward the back, on either side of each pin, about 1^1/$_2$″ from the pin. In this way, with eight tucks, you will be fitting the crown into the band that has been cut just for the wearer's head (Fig. 5–13*b*). Baste that band in place. Place the second band on the inside of the hat, right side of band to the wrong side of hat inside. It will be in the same upright position. Baste a second row in the same place as first band. Stitch, making ^{1}/$_4$″ seam.

Step 4. Fold the two bands downward. Press. Fold both raw edges of the bands ^{1}/$_4$″ toward the wrong side, baste, and press (Fig. 5–13*c*). Center the peak seam allowance inside the two bands at the ^{1}/$_4$″ folded edge at the front of the hat. Baste all the way around, then topstitch all the way around this lower edge, using rather small stitches (twelve to fifteen stitches to the inch).

KNIT TURBAN

Add a little magic to your wardrobe for every season. The small wrapped turban in its caress of gathers does many jobs. In winter-weight jersey, it keeps the head warm. In stretch terry, it covers wet tresses and curler-ridden hair for summer swim parties. In matte jerseys and metallic knits it adds a touch of mystery to every costume. The yardage may be minimum but the glamorous effect is maximum (see color Fig. 8 of red jersey and Fig. 5–14).

MATERIALS

Very thin stretch knit, 22^1/$_2$″ x 16″. Cut a rectangle with its greatest stretch along the 22^1/$_2$″ length.

ASSEMBLY

Step 1. Fold in half, right sides together, across the 16″ width. Following Fig. 5–15, stitch in a ^{1}/$_4$″ seam at bottom A, forming a tube. Then stitch in a ^{1}/$_4$″ seam across top fold B. Finally, stitch a ^{1}/$_4$″ seam along one end of the tube C.

Step 2. Fold the remaining raw edge D back 1″, then 1″ again, and tack to the inside with tacks spaced about 2″ apart.

Step 3. With heavy-duty thread or a double length of thread, about 8″ long and knotted at the end, place a row of gathering stitches along the top and the bottom seams—points A and B. Start working from point C on the inside, stopping at the folded and tacked edge D. Draw the thread into a gather about 2″ long, *not* including the folded-back edge, and secure permanently. Jeweled clip, bow, or tab can be added.

Fig. 5–14   Turban, made of wool and synthetic knit.

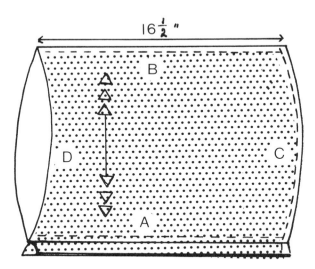

Fig. 5–15   Fold knit in half for seaming.

THE SNAIL

Snail is the popular name given to a hat that looks like it wraps the head in fabric and culminates at the back in a sash tie. There are two ways to make the hat. Both hats take off from one basic pattern and lend themselves to soft, lightweight fabrics.

The styling of the *tie-back* shell simulates a fitted cap of fabric over the hair, ending

Fig. 5–16   Snail made
of polyester jersey.

in what looks like a tie at the back of the head, but in actuality is a mock sash tie, making
the hat fit more comfortably (see color Fig. 8, white satin hat).

The *snail* is generally made of soft knit and is trimmed with a rolled band of self fabric. This styling gives height and width to the face (see Fig. 5–16 and color Fig. 13, gray
wool hat). Both look good in summer cottons, lightweight jerseys (as shown), sheer knits,
dressy weaves, such as challis, crepe, or satin (as shown). Do not use heavy fabrics.

MATERIALS

fabric: *tie back* (woven or knit), 22″ x 35″; *snail* (knit), 28″ x 42″
6″ piece of elastic, 1/4″ wide
batting: 18″ x 8″ for snail styling (optional)

PREPARATION

Make hat pattern, seam allowance included, from pattern piece A (Fig. 5–17a). This
is half of the pattern. The small tab to be tied onto the back of the hat is pattern piece B,
for tie-back shell. For snail, cut a piece of fabric 5″ wide by 42″ long (note greatest
stretch), from pattern piece C.

ASSEMBLY

Step 1. To make basic hat, place pattern piece A on fold with greatest stretch across
the 22″ width at fold. Cut. Indicate darts and stitch in four darts on the wrong side of fabric. If darts appear bulky, trim out and press open. Fold the long oval piece A in half,
right sides together, and stitch 1/4″ from raw edge, leaving a small 3″ opening as indicated
in Fig. 5–17b. Pull hat to the right side through the opening and press. Stitch opening
closed with hidden slipstitch.

Step 2. On the right side, run a row of stitches, with a loose tension on the machine,
1/2″ away from the edge (Fig. 5–17c). With small scissors, cut an opening in fold in the

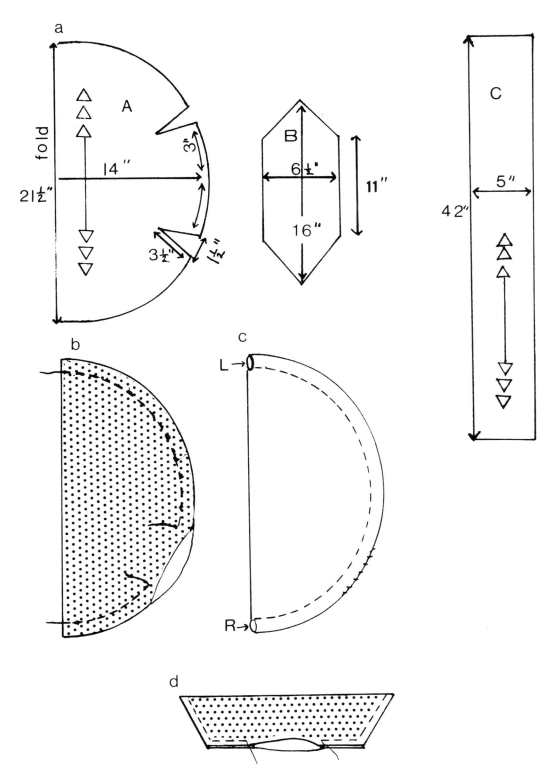

Fig. 5–17 Making the snail a. Half-pattern for snail, with small piece marked B for tie and long piece marked C for rolled top, as shown in Fig. 5–16. b. Fold pattern piece A in half, right sides together, and stitch 1/4″ from the edge, leaving open to turn right .side-out. c. On the right side, stitch 1/2″ from edge only at the rounded perimeter. d. Stitch around the raw edge perimeter of the tie, leaving an opening.

seam allowance just made at points L and R. Thread the elastic in the tunnel from point L to R. Draw elastic together and overlap ¹/₄″; secure permanently. Hat will form by itself, with a little circle of gathers in the back (see Fig. 5–18).

Step 3. To make pattern piece B, fold in half lengthwise, right sides together and stitch around raw edge. Leave opening 2″ wide (Fig. 5–17d). Turn to the right side, through the opening. Press and stitch remaining opening closed with hidden slipstitch. Fold tab over elastic at back and tie a small double knot in a decorative manner. An option would be to make this tab longer and tie a bow, or stitch on a tailored bow.

Step 4. To make the roll-top trim on the snail, cut a piece of fabric 5″ by 42″ (pattern C). The greatest stretch should be along the 42″ length. Fold in half lengthwise and stitch across the ends, right sides together, and 18″ toward the center. Repeat for the other side. Turn to right side through the opening in the center. If you have batting material, center inside this freshly made band. Close opening with a hidden slipstitch. Start to twist gently until only 5″ of plain fabric appears on the ends. It is best to do this on the ironing board. This should twist down to reach around the hat about 2″ from the center front, sloping down to the elastic at points L and R. Twist will be tacked to the hat to hold it in place and the untwisted 5″ at either end will be tied at the nape of the neck. Use Fig. 5–18 as a guide.

The batting is an optional feature. It makes the top of the twisted portion a little thicker.

VARIATIONS

Many variations can be added to this basic hat. A long, sheer 24″ x 18″ scarf can be tied in back, bands of flowers can ring the hat for a spring or wedding cap look, or a large bow can be tacked up against the back, preferably in a contrasting color.

Fig. 5–18   Back of snail, with tails of roll untied.

MINI-MADCAP MARVELS

Two versions are given for knits only, designed with a double thickness of fabric for real warmth. Long and short variations can be made on one pattern theme, with or without the addition of the long winding scarf for the young person or winter sports enthusiast (Fig. 5–19). It's shown here in its short, head-hugging styling in double-knit wool trimmed with a white felt flower (Fig. 5–20 and color Fig. 1).

MATERIALS

Use stretch knit fabric only. The stretch should be across the 22″ width of the material. Short head-hugging cap style is 22″ wide by 24″ long (finished length, 12″). The long version is 22″ wide by 30″ to 50″ long. (Finished length will be one half the length chosen.) Scarf is 16″ wide by 54″ to 66″ long (66″ will wrap once around the neck and come to the average woman's hipline).

Assorted fringe and yarn trims are purchased at the crafter's discretion. For a small supply of yarn, a card of wool used for mending socks can be purchased in most variety stores. Craft and yarn shops sell crewel yarn by the strand in magnificent colors. Felt sold in small squares can be found in fabric and variety stores for making flowers. Reread information on trims (see Fig. 5–4). Special sizing note: For small children, make the hats 18″; for teenage boys and men, measure the head, as it may be up to 24″.

Fig. 5–19 Mini-madcap marvel: long version with self scarf. Sweater-knit hat trimmed with variegated yarn tassel and scarf trimmed with variegated yarn fringe.

Fig. 5–20 Mini-madcap marvel: short head-hugging style in wool double knit, trimmed with buttonhole stitching and felt flower.

ASSEMBLY: SHORT HEAD-HUGGING STYLE

Cut a fabric so that the stretch is across the width and adjust the length to meet the needs of the hat being worked on (Fig. 5–21a).

Step 1. Fold in half lengthwise, right sides together, sew a ¼″ seam the length, forming a long tube. Press seam open (Fig. 5–21b).

Step 2. Draw up one raw end of the tube to meet the other raw end, wrong sides together, keeping the long seam flat against its counterpart. Try on at this point, placing the fold around the head. If it is not snug enough, increase the seam width until it fits snugly, but not too tight.

Step 3. Flatten the tube in half, making four layers. It will be about 11″ wide. Find the center of the 11″ piece, place a pin through all four layers, then place a pin 2″ to the left of the center pin and a third pin 2″ to the right of the center (Fig. 5–21c). Against the two folded sides, measure down 8″ and place a pin on each fold (Fig. 5–21d). Stitch, starting at the righthand pin at the top and finish at the pin on the righthand side fold. Make the seam through the four layers rather rounded, as the head is rather rounded. Repeat for the lefthand side (Fig. 5–21c). Cut away the excess, as you would trim out a dart on any heavy fabric. Press seams open and note that you will have the 4″ opening at the top.

Step 4. Fold the hat in the opposite direction, placing the right side of the newly made dart against the other newly made dart. Use Fig. 5–21d as a guide. Again, measure 8″ down on each fold line. Place the final closing seam in a similar curved manner, by sewing from the first pin to the top, closing the opening, and back down again to the second pin. This seam will look like a dome shape. Trim out this seam and turn and wear. You will note that the hat as shown allows for turning back the lower folded edge to form a cuff around the head. Study the closeup of flowers at rim and buttonhole stitch that trims the edge in Fig. 5–20.

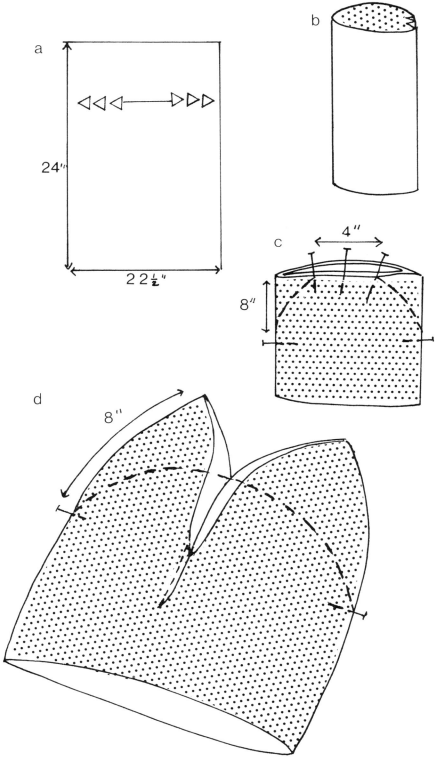

a 24" 22½"

b

c 4" 8"

d 8"

Fig. 5–21   a. Judging the stretch for main pattern piece. b. Making the initial tube. c. Pinning and stitching the tube. d. Final stitching on the tube.

ASSEMBLY: LONG MADCAP

The longer version is made basically the same. The top of the head will not have to be fitted, as in the smaller version, because the end of the hat hangs away from the crown of the head. The seam at the top of the hat need not be rounded, but may be straight. The straighter seams give a sharper, more tailored look. If you wish to have a tassel or pom-pom on the hat, it should be placed inside the hat, with its raw end sticking into the seam allowance before finishing step 4.

SCARF

Fold fabric in half lengthwise, right sides together; stitch $1/4''$ to $1/2''$ seam. Turn to the right side, keeping the seam at one side of the tube, and press. Fold remaining raw edges to the wrong side and stitch by hand with hidden slipstitch.

Fringe with long strands of yarn, placing four or five separate strands through one spot and tying in a knot at bottom of scarf. Place each set of yarns about 1" apart. An alternate trim would be to purchase fringe by the yard, six times the width of the end of the scarf. Cut in half and baste a triple fold of fringe together. Fold in seam allowance at the bottom of the scarf, place the fringe into the open end, and stitch by hand or machine to secure permanently.

FUR TOQUE

The toque style lends itself beautifully to the fake furs of today. The pattern given here is very easy to make and very warm (Fig. 5–22). The fabric backing needs to be

Fig. 5–22 Toque in white, minklike fake fur.

rather firm, as it lines itself. Reread the information given in Chapter One on working with fake furs for the fine details and tricks of working with furs. All ¹/₄″ seam allowances are included in patterns given. See color Fig. 1, white short-haired fake fur.

MATERIALS

¹/₂ yard of 50″ wide fake fur

Cut the side crown 15″ wide by 26″ long for a medium-size 22″ to 22¹/₂″ head size. Note the pile direction of the fur and indicate on the back of the piece. The fur direction should run down the width of the side crown. The crown is a complete circle of fabric with an 8″ diameter (this includes the ¹/₄″ seam allowance). The pile should run from the back of the hat to the front, indicated on the wrong side of the crown. If you desire to make the hat a little bigger, then cut the side crown 27″ by 15″, and the crown 9″ in diameter. After cutting, trim ¹/₄″ of the pile from the seam allowance.

ASSEMBLY

Step 1. Fold the side crown in half, right sides together, and seam the two 15″ ends together, making a long fur tube.

Step 2. With the right sides together, place the round crown inside the tube, forming the side crown. Baste very carefully, keeping the circular shape of the crown (Fig. 5–23). It must be noted here that most fake furs have a knitted back and there is a natural

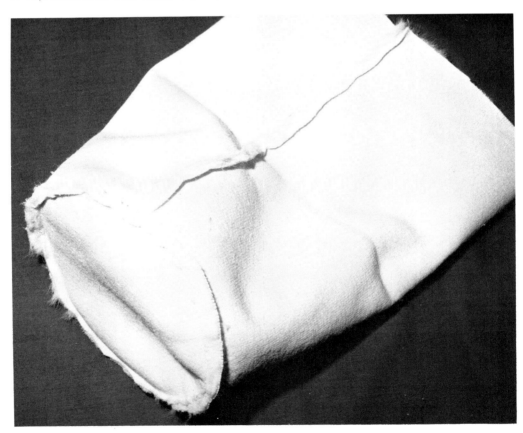

Fig. 5–23   Inside view of seams of fur toque.

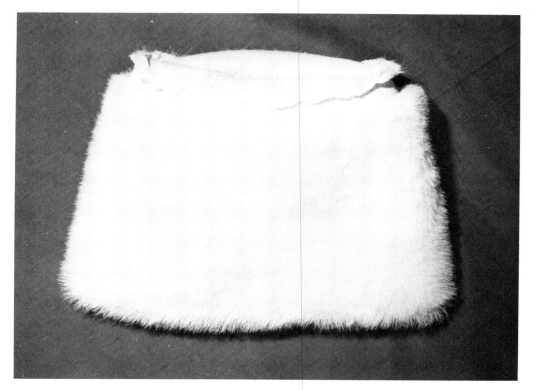

Fig. 5–24   Turn raw edge back against the inside, wrong sides together.

tendency to stretch the seam allowance of the side crown when fitting it to the round upper crown. After this has been pinned and basted in place, stitch permanently, working on the crown rather than the side crown.

Step 3. With the hat still wrong-side-out, turn half the 15″ width of the side crown back against itself, wrong sides together. The raw edge of the side crown will touch the seam of the circumference of the crown. Try on for adjustments. Secure with hand stitches to the seam allowance around the crown (Fig. 5–24). If the hat appears too high for you, then just cut off an inch at a time from the bottom edges of the side crown before folding back to begin step 3.

Turn out and enjoy this warm, lightweight fur hat.

VARIATIONS

This can be made for a child, using a 7″-diameter crown. It would need a side crown 10″ deep by 21½″ wide.

ENGLISH AUTO HAT

This versatile pattern can be made into many stylings to suit mode and need of men and women with just a change of fabric. (See Figs. 5–25, 5–26, and color Figs. 7 and 10.) The crown is made up of eight wedge-shaped pieces, with a partial band and a peak added. That is all there is to the basic construction. It's the styling that counts. If the fabric is rather stiff and firm, the crown will stand up smartly, holding its sporty shape. If the styling is made of soft but closely woven fabric, such as a lightweight wool or a crisp sport

Fig. 5–25 English auto hat for women in assorted calico prints—a good opportunity for the crafter to use remnants.

Fig. 5–26 English auto hat for men in small-plaid wool.

fabric, the crown is pulled forward and tacked permanently to the peak. The flat squashy look is very sporty and rather dashing. It is worn close down over the forehead, more typical of the way a man would wear it.

MATERIALS

>   outside fabric: $1/2$ yard of 45″
>   lining: $1/2$ yard of 45″ for inside hat
>   crown interlining: $1/2$ yard of 30″ (lightweight)
>   peak interlining: 12″ by 12″ (Permette preferred)
>   grosgrain ribbon: 24″ by 1″ wide

If you would like to use an outside fabric that is not strong, it can be backed with a heavy interlining. Good fabrics are wools, flat knits, denims, duck, linen, suede cloth, cottons such as poplin, pique, gingham, and seersucker.

PREPARATION

Copy the pattern in Fig. 5–27 for the crown wedges. For woman's hat, use as is: It includes $1/4$″ seam allowance. For man's hat, add the $1/4$″ seam allowance to pattern given. Cut eight wedges from the outside fabric, eight interlining pieces, if needed, and eight lining pieces (optional). Using peak pattern in Fig. 5–8, cut two from outside fabric and one from firm interlining. All hats will look more finished with a lining, but it is not a necessity if the fabric and interlining are firm.

ASSEMBLY

Step 1. Begin by basting all the wedge-shaped interlinings against the wrong side of the outside fabric for each wedge. Place two of the wedges right sides together, and begin stitching from the bottom to the point. Sew two more wedges, then join the first four. Repeat for the other four wedges. Notch, trim, and press open seams over a presser's mitt or rolled towel. Return to the machine and topstitch $1/8$″ from the seam on both sides (Fig. 5–28*a*). Repeat for the other four wedges and join the two halves together. Before finally topstitching this last seam, try the hat on and make sure you can only fit one thumb under its perimeter when on the head. Make any adjustment in the two seams before topstitching. Make the lining without all the additional topstitching. Slip into the outer shell, wrong sides together. Baste perimeter.

Step 2. For the peak, place the two outside fabrics right side together, making two layers. Stitch around the large outside edge only, notch seam allowance, and press. Slip the interlining, without seam allowance, between the wrong sides of the peak. Topstitch one or two rows with matching thread, $1/4$″ to $3/4$″ off newly sewn edge. This will help give support and strength to the peak. An alternate method for making the peak is to use two interlinings. Place the outside peak pieces right sides together; place both interlinings on top; stitch around the large outer curve, notch, turn outside fabrics to the outside, and press. Set aside.

Step 3. Make the partial band by cutting a length of outside fabric and interlining material, both 1″ by 13″. Place the interlining against the wrong side of the partial band, fold in half, covering the interlining, and baste the edges closed. Fold the band in half lengthwise and find the center. Mark with a pin. Place the pin against the seam of one of the wedges. This will be the center back of the hat. The band will not reach completely around the crown. Ease the band off the raw edges of the crown and trim excess (Fig. 5–28*a*). Baste in place.

Step 4. Center and baste the peak against the front of the hat, placing ends of the

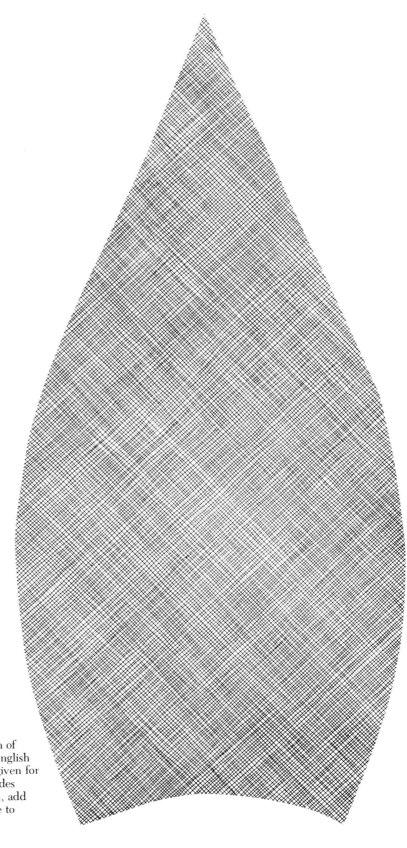

Fig. 5–27   Pattern of
crown wedge for English
auto hat. Pattern given for
women's hat; includes
$^1/_4''$ seam. For men, add
$^1/_4''$ seam allowance to
pattern given.

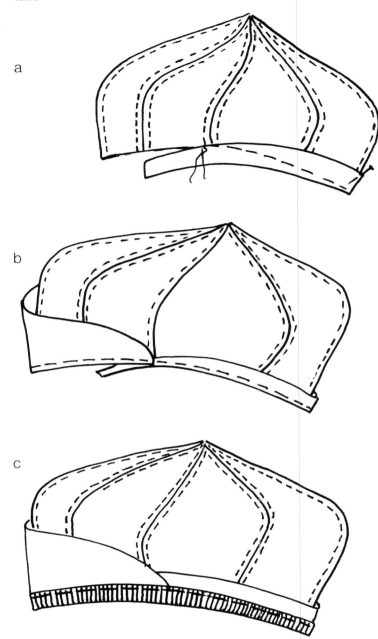

a

b

c

Fig. 5–28 Assembling
the auto hat a. Placing on
the partial band. Note
the stitching on each side
of each wedge. b. Plac-
ing the peak over the
end of the partial band.
Trim out excess. c. Plac-
ing the grosgrain ribbon
on edge of hat below raw
edge of hat, band, and
peak.

peak over the ends of the partial band. Baste against the raw edges of the upper shell.
Stitch peak and band permanently to crown, $1/4''$ from the edge all the way around the hat
(Fig. 5–28b). Keep the hat in position with peak folded up. Notch seam allowance.

    Step 5. Pin one edge of the grosgrain ribbon around the raw edge of the hat, starting
from the center back and lapping over the starting point. The edge of the ribbon will be
placed on the seam line. Start and finish with a lapped fold of ribbon at center back. A
second row of stitches will be placed just on the edge of the ribbon, catching the ribbon
to the seam allowance (Fig. 5–28c). This will serve as a covering for raw edges of the seam
allowance. Press the ribbon to the inside.

SOFT KNIT BERET

This little cutie, shown in Fig. 5–29 and color Fig. 1, can be made from very little fabric, as it uses the pattern for the eight wedges of the English auto cap (see Fig. 5–27). The stretch should be across the width of the wedge. Cut a band 3″ wide by the circumference of your head, plus ¼″ seam allowance on each end. The stretch should be along the length, not across, the 3″ width. Omit the lining and interlining.

Fig. 5–29 Soft knit beret of double knit.

a

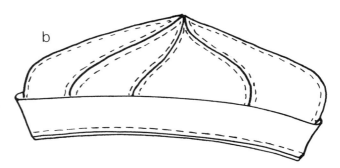

b

Fig. 5–30 a. Fold 3″-wide circular band in half. b. Place raw edges of band against raw edge of hat. Stitch all the way around.

MATERIALS

    ¹/₃ yard of 45″ wide: flat knit or low-ribbed sweater knit preferred

ASSEMBLY

    Step 1. Prepare as in step 1 for the English auto cap, without lining.

    Step 2. Fold band in half crosswise, placing right sides together, and stitch the seam, attaching the two 3″ ends. Fold the circle band in half lengthwise, right sides together, and press (Fig. 5–30a). Place the circle of the band with its double raw edges against the right side of the hat, stretching and easing the band where necessary. Stitch permanently (Fig. 5–30b). Turn the seam to the inside and you are ready to go, with the band hugging the head.

    If you want to make this hat from a woven material, cut the band on the true bias. It will take 1 yard of fabric, 45″ wide.

CLASSIC FRENCH BERET

    A hat that is of impeccable taste in all the fashion capitals of the world is this beret. It is one of the few hats that will go with any outfit. It looks best in dressy fabrics like velvet, challis, soft wools, smooth-surfaced knits, linen, silk surah, or heavy satin. The hat is worn to one side of the head and crushed gently (Fig. 5–31 and color Fig. 8). It can be trimmed with a ribbon cockade or a beautiful mock buckle or clasp. This pattern is

Fig. 5–31   Classic French beret in velvet.

Fig. 5–32 Side crown pattern: two pieces to form lower half. Trace two halves; form a single piece by placing the double lines of one over the other. This is half the pattern for the side crown. The upper crown is just a circle with a 12″ diameter.

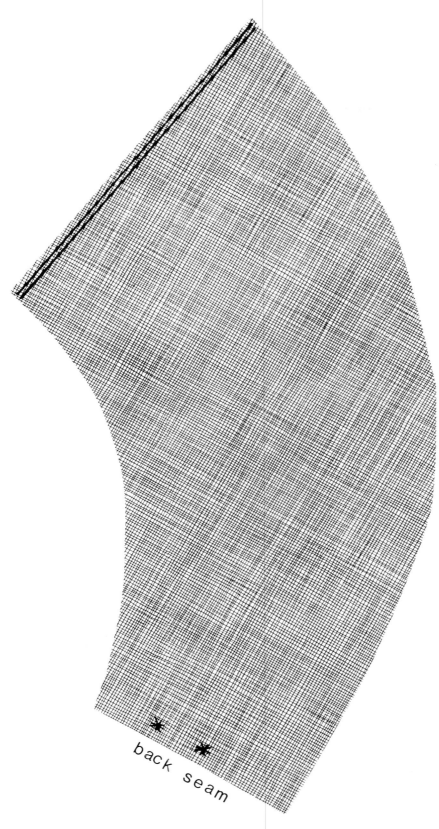

back seam

Fig. 5–32 continued.

worked for a 22" head size. If your head is bigger, cut $1/8"$ at a time away from the seam allowance on the smaller curve of the lower crown portion. Cut the patterns, noting the grain lines. Only two pattern pieces are required ($1/4"$ seams are included).

MATERIALS

outside: 18" by 30"
lining: 18" by 30"
woven bias interfacing: $11/2"$ by 26" long
grosgrain ribbon: 1" by 25" (color should match outer fabric)

PREPARATION

Cut an even upper circle with a diameter of 12" for crown: cut one from the outside fabric and one from the lining fabric. Cut one curved lower portion from the outside fabric and one from the lining (Fig. 5–32). To enable us to give this large-size pattern in this comfortable text, the lower section is shown split in half, rather than have to scale it down. Place the double line of one piece over its matching mate to make one-half of a crescent-shaped pattern piece for the side crown. This is only half the pattern. Note where this is to be placed on a fold, and note the grain line.

ASSEMBLY

Step 1. Begin by placing the two short ends, point ** of the side crown portion, with right sides together. Make $1/4"$ seam. Press. Repeat for the lining.

Step 2. Place the side crown portion of the outside fabric over the round top portion, baste, and seam $1/4"$ from the circular edge all the way around. Repeat for the lining. Press seam open over a tailor's ham or a presser's mitt, or place on a sleeve board or a rolled-up towel. Replace in the machine and run two rows of stitches very carefully $1/8"$ off each edge of the newly made seam. This additional seaming gives the hat some body and helps to hold the perky shape. Study Figs. 5–33 and 5–34 and you will see this double

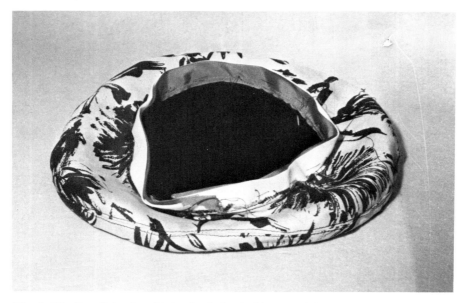

Fig. 5–33   Interlining band (white) is behind ribbon. Both have been attached permanently to the raw edge of hat and lining. This is a view of the hat with lining side out.

Fig. 5–34   Ribbon is turned to the inside of hat. Note that hat will not lie flat.

row of stitches. Do the same for the lining and slip into the outside hat, wrong sides together. Baste the two rims together.

Step 3. You will note that the lower portion of the beret does not lie flat against the upper portion. This is intentional, as the shape of the lower portion helps to hold the hat away from the face. Try hat on. If the circumference of the lower crown is too small, enlarge by cutting off ⅛″ all the way around. Try on and repeat if necessary. Trim out lining, too.

Step 4. Notch the perimeter of the two raw edges ⅛″ deep every 1½″. Cut a strip of woven interfacing on the bias 1½″ by 26″. Fold in half. Baste the two raw edges of the interlining band to one edge of the ribbon, placing stitches close to edge. The interfacing should be hidden by the ribbon. Beginning at the center back seam, baste the edge of the ribbon with the two raw edges of interlining basted against it, to the right side of the hat and its lining, no more than ¼″ deep (Fig. 5–33). The rest of the ribbon will be sticking up from the hat perimeter. Fold the end, overlap the back, and trim off what is unnecessary. Using your zipper foot, permanently stitch ⅛″ from the edge of the ribbon, using your basting line as a guide. Notch the seam allowance of the outer shell and the lining to ease. Place a second row of stitches ⅛″ deeper to hold ribbon inside the hat. Ribbon is not generally tacked to the inside. It goes to the inside when you put the hat on (Fig. 5–34).

CLOCHE

This is a hat with a six-piece crown and a shaped brim. The brim is a versatile one that allows the hat to be worn three ways—down for the cloche feeling, as in Fig. 5–35 and color Fig. 13). This way, the hat is pulled down and the brim frames the face. The hat may have the brim flipped up in the back and worn low over the eyes as an active sport hat. The front brim can be turned back against the crown and tacked, like the popular flapper style of the 30s.

Fig. 5–35   Cloche in washable velvet with pinned-on flower.

MATERIALS

> outside: ³/₄ yard at 45″
> lining: ¹/₃ at 45″
> interlining: ³/₄ yard at 45″ (for brim—rather firm)
> grosgrain ribbon: 1″ by 24″
> optional outside trim: flowers, ribbons, etc.

PREPARATION

Cut paper pattern from Figs. 5–36 and 5–37, adding ¹/₄″ seam allowance. Cut six crown pieces each from outside fabric, lining, and interlining. To enable us to give the large-size brim pattern in this comfortable text, it is split in half, rather than have to scale the pattern down (Fig. 5–37). Place the double line over its matching mate to make one-half of a crescent-shaped pattern for the brim. Cut two brim pieces from outside fabric and one interlining. Study 5–38*a* for layout suggestion.

ASSEMBLY

Step 1: Cut the pie-shaped crown wedges, adhering to the pattern given, noting the curve of the edges (Fig. 5–36). This will create a nice, rounded crown when finished, with a head size approximately 22¹/₂″. Baste each piece of crown interlining against the wrong side of each crown piece. Stitch three of the crown pieces together, notch seam

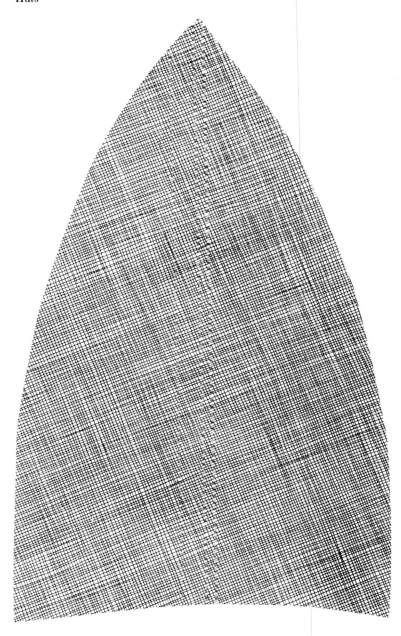

Fig 5–36   Cloche
crown wedge pattern.
Add ¼″ seam allowance.

allowance, and press. Repeat for the second set of three crown pieces. Then stitch the
two halves together. To give a sporty look, topstitching may be applied ⅛″ inch on each
side of each seam of the crown. Make the lining exactly as the outside and place the lining
in the crown, wrong sides together. Baste in place around edge. Try on for adjustment,
then set aside.

    Step 2. Having cut two outside fabric pieces for the brim and one interlining, lightly
place the brim pieces around the crown, testing to see that they fit snugly. Seam each of
the above pieces at back seam (Fig. 5–37) to form three complete circular pieces. Press
seams open. Place the right sides of the two outside pieces together; place the interlining

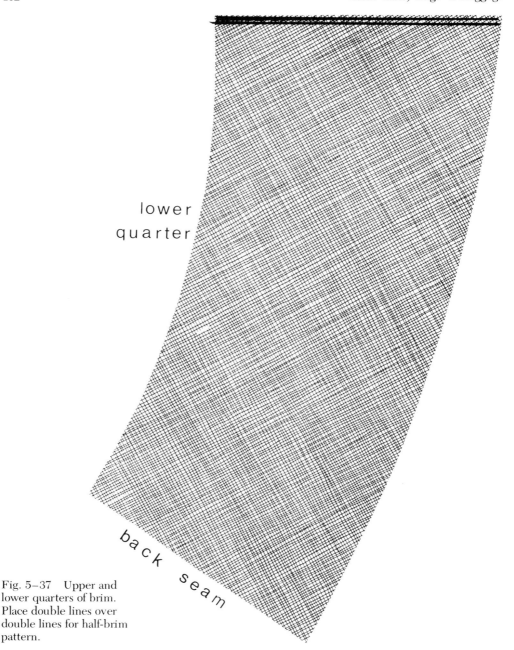

Fig. 5–37   Upper and
lower quarters of brim.
Place double lines over
double lines for half-brim
pattern.

over the wrong side of one of the outside pieces. Stitch through the three pieces of fabric
along the seam line of the wide outer rim of the brim, notch, turn, and press (Fig.
5–38*b*). Add a row of topstitching $^1/_4''$ to $^1/_2''$ along the outer edges of the newly turned
brim.

  Step 3. Turn the crown right-side-out. Position center back seam of brim at any seam
line of the crown, placing remaining portions of the brim outside, matching the circumference of the brim with that of the crown (Fig. 5–39). Using a $^1/_4''$ seam, baste the brim
raw edges to the crown with outside fabric of the crown against the outside fabric of the

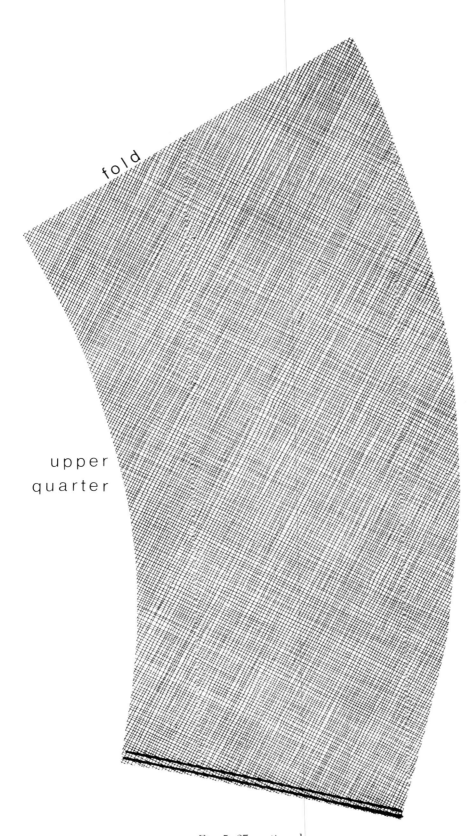

Fig. 5–37 continued.

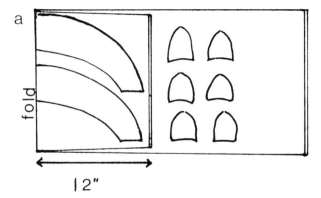

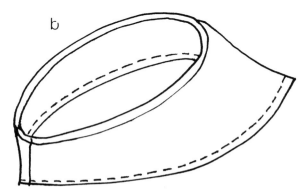

Fig. 5–38 Making the cloche a. Layout. Fold back one selvage to fit half the crown. Cut wedges individually. b. Topstitch brim before placing on crown.

brim. This is a good time to try on the hat for fit, or brim adjustment. Stitch around the entire circle of the crown, $^1/_4$″ off the raw edges (Fig. 5–40).

Step 4. Without turning out the brim and crown, pin and baste one edge of the grosgrain ribbon over the newly made seam on the brim side of the two units. The other edge of the ribbon will stand up out of the hat (see Figs. 5–39 and 5–40). Begin the ribbon at the center back and end the ribbon with a folded end overlapping the starting point. The ribbon edge will barely lap over the newly made seam. With zipper foot, stitch on top of the ribbon $^1/_8$″ off the edge, attaching ribbon onto seam allowance. This will catch the crown, lining, and brim again, but its purpose is to cover the raw edges of the seams and make a neat lining in the hat. Flip the hat to the right side and the ribbon will flip to the inside. Tack the ribbon in three evenly separated places through the crown lining into the seam allowances of the outer crown (never through to the outer portion of the crown). It's now ready to wear.

VARIATIONS

Additional trim may be added at this time. Ribbon around lower crown, flowers, feathers, scarf tied and left flapping, bows (see Fig. 5–4). It is suggested that a long needle, such as a "milliner," be used, making as few stitches as possible.

Adjustments can be made at every step in this hat. The crown can be made smaller, the brim can be made narrower, particularly if you have a short neck. Take a deeper seam in the back where brim attaches to crown. Adjust until it feels comfortable.

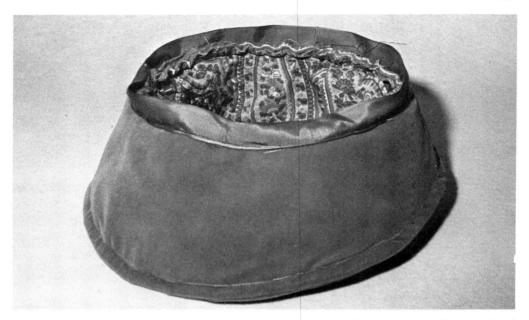

Fig. 5–39 Brim placed over the crown portion and seamed together. Grosgrain ribbon is placed over ¼″ seam in an upright position and stitched on the edge, just beyond the ¼″ seam holding brim to crown.

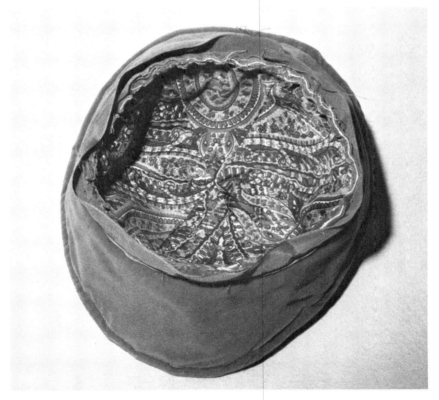

Fig. 5–40 Looking down into crown at linings. Note how grosgrain ribbon stands up. It will be tucked into the hat and tacked to lining at front and both sides.

UNISEX INTERNATIONAL FUR HAT

This traditional styling is good looking for both men and women. It is usually made in fake lamb's wool, caracul, or mouton fur. Note that these furs do not have a distinct pile direction (Fig. 5–41).

MATERIALS

    $^1/_4$ yard of fake fur, 50″ wide
    $^1/_4$ yard of 54″ winter lining that is rather firm, such as Sunback, or quilted satin or
        firm satin (or $^1/_2$ yard at 45″)
    grosgrain ribbon: $^1/_2$″ wide by 24″ long, to match lining

PREPARATION

Pattern is very easy for this hat, planned for a medium-size 22″ head and including $^1/_4$″ seam allowance. Upper crown will be formed from a rectangle 11$^1/_2$″ long by 7″ high. Round off the corners on only *one* end of the rectangle (Fig. 5–42a). Cut two upper crowns from pattern out of fake fur and cut two for the lining. The second piece is the band, which will be 23″ long by 4$^1/_2$″ deep. Cut one from the fake fur and one from the lining. See layout instructions in Fig. 5–42b. For a larger head size, the band will have to equal the lower two pieces of the upper crown and seam allowance.

Fig. 5–41 Unisex international hat of fake fur.

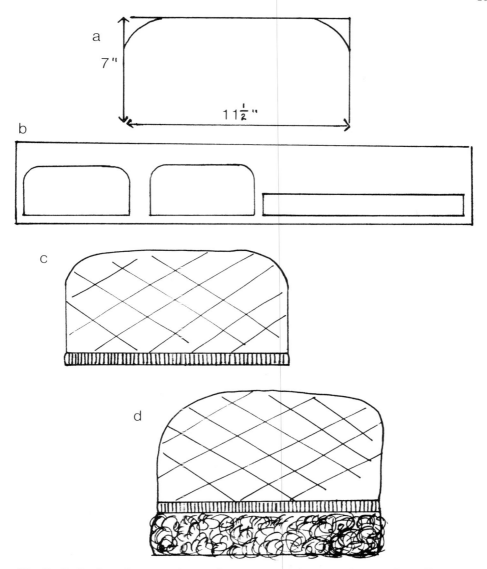

Fig. 5–42 Making the unisex hat a. Shape pattern from rectangle, rounding off top corners gently. b. Layout on fake fur for two crown pieces and band. c. Place a band of ribbon around the edge of lining, stitching edge of ribbon to edge of outer shell and lining. d. Place raw edge of fur band between the outside and the edge of ribbon, keeping fur of band on same side as lining, to be flipped to right side later.

ASSEMBLY

Step 1. With right sides together, seam the rounded portions of the two upper crowns together. Repeat for the lining. Place the ribbon around the perimeter of the lining so that the lower portion is $1/8''$ below the raw edge of the lining on the right side. Topstitch all the way around, lapping the back (Fig. 5–42c). With wrong sides together, fit the lining into the outer shell of the upper crown. Turn so the lining is right-side-out, with fur to the inside. Set aside.

Step 2. With right sides together, stitch the short ends of the band fur together. Repeat for the lining. Press seams open. With right sides together, place the lining into

Fig. 5–43 Sundowner
hat of white muslin,
trimmed with applique,
and matching classic tote
bag. *Made by Lorna
Blauvelt*

the circle of fur and stitch along one edge only. Turn to the right side and press. Baste the lining to the wrong side.

Step 3. With the hat placed before you, lining outward on the crown, slip the two remaining raw edges of the band between the outside and the edge of the ribbon attached to the lining. Note that the fur of the band is against the grosgrain ribbon. Baste through all four layers (Fig. 5–42*d*). Turn the hat to the outside, flipping the band portion back against the outer fur. Try on for final fitting. Flip band down to a sewing position and top-stitch the edges of the band along the ribbon. Turn to the outside, press an indentation across the top of the hat, causing a squaring off of the top, and enjoy the cold days.

SUNDOWNER

For complete, umbrella protection from the sun, the sundowner is a must. Shown in color, Fig. 10, in white muslin with applique and matching bag, this versatile hat can be made in dressy materials to accompany dresses for weddings, garden parties, and outdoor graduations. Additions of artifical flowers, ribbons, and scarves in place of the applique add to the lighthearted effect of this hat. It combines two patterns—the brim of the open-crown brimmer and the crown of the cloche. If the hat is made of a cotton-blend fabric for sportswear, it needs no lining or interlining (Fig. 5–43).

MATERIALS

³/₄ yard of 45″ outer fabric
³/₄ yard of 45″ interlining
25″ of bias binding, ¹/₂″ to ³/₄″ wide

ASSEMBLY

Step 1. Copy pattern for the brim of the open-crown brimmer. Proceed to make the brim only, following step 2 under open-crown brimmer.

Step 2. Copy the pattern for the six-piece crown of the cloche (Fig. 5–36). Make the crown. Follow step 1 under cloche instructions.

Step 3. Place the right side of the brim against the right side of the crown (Fig. 5–44). Pin to make sure they fit. If the brim is too small, trim ¹/₈″ at a time away from the inside raw edge. When both edges fit together, place one edge of the bias binding against the edge of the brim. Stitch around the hat, catching both the layers of the brim with the edges of the crown and the edge of the bias binding. Fold the binding toward the inside of the crown, covering the raw edges of crown and brim. Baste the other folded edge of the binding against the inside of the crown, then machine stitch permanently. Overlap the binding at the back of the hat with a diagonal fold.

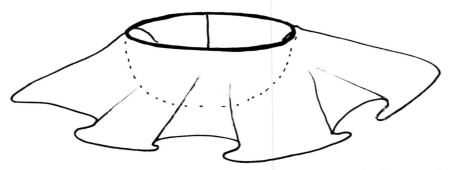

Fig. 5–44   Place brim against inverted six-piece crown. Stitch bias binding around raw edge of brim and crown. Dotted lines indicate the crown inverted under the brim.

Glossary

Applique: The art of applying small pieces of fabric to a background of fabric to create a pictorial type of decoration.

Bandeau: Small open-crown head cover.

Basting: Temporary stitches used to hold two or more layers of fabric together before final stitching.

Batting: Any filler placed between the top and bottom layers of fabric, generally for the purpose of quilting. In handbags, the batting serves only a decorative purpose. In hat making, the batting can be used for warmth.

Beret: Soft crushed hat worn generally to the side of crown, mostly for its decorative value and sometimes for minimum warmth.

Bias: The diagonal (45-degree angle) intersecting of the crosswise and lengthwise threads of a given piece of fabric.

Brim: The part of a hat that extends beyond the crown of the hat and generally stretches out or is folded back against the crown.

Cloche: Classic French name for a hat made of a number of sections. It covers the crown and has a brim (shaped or round) worn downward to frame the face.

Closure: Anything used to hold a handbag or piece of luggage closed, such as a zipper, Velcro, or buckles.

Colorfast: Fabric that has been treated so the color will not come out in washing.

Cording: See Piping.

Cowl: Soft circular drape of fabric around the head.

Crosswise: The measurement across the narrowest width.

Crown: The top of a hat covering top of the head.

Dart: A shaping technique to give fullness. Fabric is folded and stitched to form a V, starting at the widest point (the seam allowance) and ending directly on the fold.

Drill: Heavy twill-weave material of narrow width (30") used in clothing construction as an interlining. Used here to interline the handbags.

English Auto Cap: Hat with a pieced soft crown and peak. Used for both warmth and to shade eyes from sun's glare.

Face: The right side of a piece of fabric.

Fake Furs: Material that looks like fur but is generally made of synthetic fibers.

Flap: The part of the handbag attached by only one edge to the back of the bag; it is loose and used to cover the opening at the top and part of the front of the bag.

Floorboards: An additional, rigid piece of hard material covered with fabric that is put into a handbag after it is finished for the purpose of making the bottom rigid or firm.

Frog: Small fabric closure made by decoratively twisting a covered cording.

Grain Line: The crosswise threads as they intersect the longer, lengthwise threads.

Grosgrain: Ribbon of a silky type that has heavy crosswise ribs.

Hardware: In the handbag industry, this covers the rigid frames, handles, closures, rings, and anything of decorative nature used to enhance the appearance of the bag that is not made of fabric.

Harness Latch: A two-piece latch consisting of a portion with a snap latch that catches on a ring. Used for animal tethers and on flagpoles.

Hood: Head covering designed for warmth and protection, covering both head and all or part of the neck.

Interlining: Layer of firm fabric between the outer fabric and the lining for the purpose of giving shape or strength to the item being made.

Knits: Fabric made by knitting yarns together rather than weaving.

Layout: Chart showing placement of pattern pieces for cutting.

Lengthwise: The measurement along the longest edge.

Lining: This is the attractive inside of a hat or bag that serves to cover all the seams and generally adds to the finished appearance.

Metallic: Any fabric with silver or gold yarns running through, or made entirely of these yarns.

Mock Buckle: An accessory that looks like a buckle but doesn't have a shank.

Monogram: Any personal initials added to an article as personal identification, generally of a decorative nature.

Needles: Betweens—short, round-eyed needles used for hand sewing with short, even stitches, such as quilting. *Sharps*—medium-length, thin needles used for general sewing.

Open-Crown Hat: Any hat that has a brim or peak, but does not cover the crown.

Patchwork: The sewing together of small pieces of fabric to form a decorative pattern.

Pattern: The various pieces of one individual project, supplied with or without seam allowances.

Peak: Portion of hat that extends from forehead for purpose of shading the eyes.

Permette: Product of Conso Co., interlining used for very firm articles.

Pile: Fabric made with noticeable yarns standing up from surface of fabric. Examples are velvet, corduroy, and fake furs.

Piping: Sometimes called *cording* or *welting*, piping is the encasing of a cord in a bias strip of fabric. It is used as a decoration in the seams of a sewn item.

Pockets: Patch—pocket with the edges turned back, sewn on three sides to fabric, used inside or outside a bag. *Private wallet pocket*—loose pocket with a zipper top for private papers. *Quickie zip-top pocket*—Zip-top pocket placed against the handbag lining.

Presser Foot: On the sewing machine, the small hinged foot that fits onto the needle bar to hold the fabric in proper position for sewing.

Presser's Mitt: An article used in tailoring round seams, like a mitten without a thumb, that is stuffed. Made of heavy drill material, it can be purchased or made at home

Quilting: The stitching that holds two layers of fabric, with a layer of batting material between, together. Can be done by hand or machine. Generally of decorative nature. Used in handbag making to strengthen the outside to the interlining.

Raw Edges: The cut edges of any piece of fabric.

Right Side: Outside of the garment or the finished side of a piece of fabric. (Also called the face of the fabric.)

Seam Allowance: Width of fabric beyond seam line. For handbags, $1/4''$ to $1/2''$ is used, for hats $1/4''$ is usually used.

Selvage: The narrow, tightly woven edge of the fabric as it comes off the bolt.

Shell: In accessory crafting, the unfinished but assembled portion of a bag or hat

Slash: To cut into seam allowance for the purpose of easing or turning a seam.

Snail: Hat that hugs the crown of the head with a large roll of fabric over the top.

Snood: Hat with a loose-fitting crown fitted onto band. Crown generally worn hanging toward the back, covering hair loosely.

Tab: A small loop attached at one end, generally to hold some part of a handbag together, such as the handles or closure.

Tack: Joining two or more layers of fabric together with a small set of hand stitches at one spot. Each tack is separate.

Ticking: Heavy twill-weave material used for making pillows, found in stripes and prints.

Topstitching: Line of stitching placed on the right side of item. Used for strengthening, shaping, and/or decoration. Could be plain running type or fancy types found on the newer machines.

Toque: Hat shaped somewhat like a drum. Worn on top of the head for decoration or pulled down over the ears for warmth.

Trainman's Hat: Fabric hat with loose upper crown and peak. Worn for protection of hair and to avert sun glare.

Trim: To cut away excess fabric.

Trimming: Ornamentation added. Could be fabrics, such as lace, rickracks, and braids or fancy buckles, buttons, chains, or closures.

Turban: Hat that is close fitting and looks like it has been wrapped around the head, as in days of old. Now made with planned gathers.

Unisex: Worn by both male and female.

Wallet Pocket: An additional pocket placed into the lining of a handbag that would have a closed top, generally used to keep one's wallet and important documents in.

Washable Belt Interfacing: Best product is a lightweight synthetic material that looks like screening.

Welting: See Piping.

Wrong Side: The side of a piece of fabric that does not have the finest finish, or the inside of a garment.

Yardage: The amount of fabric required for making an individual article.

Sources of Supply

The materials for hat and handbag making are readily available, but widely dispersed among stores such as retail fabric stores, department stores, drapery supply stores, trimming stores, and even variety stores. (Don't forget your own scrap basket.) It is suggested that, when looking for a specific trim seen in the text, you bring your text along, as sometimes names of products may vary.

Quilt Batting

There are two main sources for batting. The Stearns & Foster Company of Cincinnati, Ohio 45215, makes the product called Mountain Mist. If you cannot find this excellent product in your area, write to the company for advice as to where you can purchase it.

Second source is the big mail-order catalogue stores. Check in the catalogues under "batts," "battings," or "quilting supplies." The third way to locate batting material is through the Yellow Pages in your telephone book. Ask for the product name, finish, thickness, size, weight, and cost. Almost all major department stores in large cities throughout the country carry this material. It is generally found in or near the piece goods department, or could be in the area where they sell yarns and needlecraft supplies. Crib size is the hardest to find. You may have to take a larger one and cut it down. Crib size is 45" x 66"; full size is 80" x 96".

Needles and Thread

Use thread products manufactured by top companies: Coats & Clark, Talon, and Belding Corticelli.

Quilting thread is a special thread not often displayed over the counter, but usually available in colors if asked for. Best hand sewing needles I have found to date are imported from England by Boye Needle Co., Chicago, Illinois.

Fabrics

Fabric stores dealing with only ready-to-wear fabric are your best source. Most will carry trimmings too. Try drapery supply stores for drapery and upholstery weight materials. The latter will carry heavy piping used in slipcovers, but call it welting.

Trimmings

Trimming supply stores carry everything from flowers to buckles to chains to interesting embroidery yarns. They are also a prime source for drill fabric.

Try local hardware stores for items such as harness snaplocks, rings, chains.

Railroad emblem patches are manufactured by Walthers, 4050 N. 34th Street, Milwaukee,

Wisconsin 53216. Local New York City Source is Polk's Hobby Shop, 314 Fifth Avenue. Also look in phone directory under model railroad suppliers. There are railroad buffs all over the country.

Specialty Items

Permette is made by Conso Products Co., Box 1001, East Station, Yonkers, New York 10704. Almost every drapery supply store will have this product.

Velcro is made by Velcro Company. Write for information to Velcro Consumer Education, 41 E. 51st Street, New York, New York 10022.

Dorothy Frager

I'm a New Yorker with a strong influence of Swedish on my maternal side. Every woman in my family learned needlecrafts from an early age and I followed that tradition, making my own clothing from the age of 15.

My teen years were filled to capacity working toward my chosen merchandising career, coupled with being a teen skating champion who made her own costumes. I attended several New York colleges, which led me to Columbia University for final degree work. After spending nine years as a clothing buyer for two major New York resident buying offices, I married, moved to northern New Jersey, and had two delightful boys.

When I was casting about for something worthwhile to work at professionally, I found my sewing and clothing construction education were in great demand in the area. Through teaching, I learned the varied needs that women sought from their encounters with needlecrafts. Some have heavy family and community commitments and need to produce a craft article in a reasonable amount of time, while others enjoy a great deal of handiwork and scheduling is of no consequence.

I first turned my attention to the old family craft of quilting, which was becoming popular. I worked at modernizing the old techniques to meet the demands of today's crafter. Seeing a need for a complete teaching text, I wrote *The Quilting Primer* for Chilton. Then the *Start off in Boutique Quilting* for Chilton, which deals mostly with small gift items, followed by *Start off in Making Cloth Handbags*. Seeing how enjoyable it was for women to stitch up small items, I began to teach a course in boutique gift items, including handbags. The demand was so great to teach the handbags that it developed into an entire eight-week course at two adult education centers in this county. With that, I turned my attention to designing more and more hats and handbags so popular today. Thus developed this book.

I'm happy to have had a hand in developing another aspect of needlecrafts for the home sewer. It's practical and, at the same time, artistic.